Australian Anglicans Remember

Charles Sherlock

Australian Anglicans Remember

First published in 2015
by Broughton Publishing Pty Ltd
32 Glenvale Crescent
Mulgrave VIC 3170

Copyright © Charles Sherlock 2015

All rights reserved. No part of this publication may be reproduced, stored in a retrieval system or transmitted, in any form or by any means electronic, photocopying, recording or otherwise, without the prior written permission of the publisher.

ISBN 978-0-9750866-5-0

Contents

January 1: The Naming and Circumcision of Jesus 3
January 1: New Year's Day 8
January 2: Eliza Hassall 11
January 6: The Epiphany of our Lord 14
January 26: Australia Day 18
February 3: First Anglican Service on Sydney Cove 21
February 20: William Grant Broughton 24
March 9: Sister Emma SSA 29
March 19: Joseph, husband of the Blessed Virgin Mary 32
April 6: Frederic Barker 35
April 8: Georgiana Molloy 40
April 11: George Augustus Selwyn 44
April 25: Anzac Day 49
May 27–June 3 Week of Prayer for Reconciliation 53
July 1: Coming of the Light 57
July 13: Sydney James Kirkby 61
August 15: Mary, Mother of our Lord 66
September 2: Martyrs of New Guinea 71
September 3: Eliza Darling 77
September 11: Mother Esther CHN 80
September 15: John Oliver Feetham 85
September 18: John Ramsden Wollaston 89
September 20: John Coleridge Patteson 93
November 2: All Souls 96
November 25: James Noble 99
December 2: Frances Perry 103

Dedication

This resource had its beginnings in the mind and heart of the Revd Dr Ronald Dowling. A long-standing member of the Liturgical Commission, he drafted the Calendar in *A Prayer Book for Australia*. As one baptised into Christ, and later ordained deacon and priest, Ron delighted in the communion of saints — with all their graced oddities — both earthly and heavenly. He passed too young from one to the other.

This small volume is dedicated to Ron. May it deepen readers' sense of our communion, with "angels and archangels and all the company of heaven", in the love and grace of the triune God.

Introduction

Many Australian Christians know little of the numerous others in this country who, by God's grace, were effective witnesses to Christ. In the first Australian Anglican prayer book, *An Australian Prayer Book (AAPB, 1977)*, a few local festivals were included — Australia Day (January 26), First Service at Sydney Cove (February 3), Anzac Day (April 25) — but not Australian people.

In *A Prayer Book for Australia (APBA, 1995)*, the Calendar included a dozen or more people in whose lives God's grace was so evident that they are commemorated in some part of this land. It also included some Festivals previously unobserved (e.g. Mary and Joseph) and allocated readings for others (e.g. New Guinea Martyrs).

Australian Anglicans Remember covers all Australian and New Zealand commemorations listed in *APBA*, and festivals not included in *AAPB*.

Each entry includes several sections.

- 'Who was ...?' draws on several sources, notably the *Australian Dictionary of Biography* (Melbourne: MU Press, 1988, now online), Unit 4 of the *Trinity Certificate in Theology and Ministry* (written by the author), and Gilbert Sinden, *Times & Seasons* (Adelaide: Open Book, 1978).
- 'Commemorations' lists known places where the person's memory is perpetuated in Australia.

'Resources for liturgical use' includes a Service introduction — which could be read aloud or included in a pew sheet — and Sentence(s), Prayer(s) and Readings. These have been chosen or composed to reflect the God-given charisms displayed in the life and ministry of the person(s) concerned. Where *APBA*, General Synod or another Province has made provision, these are followed.

Saints and Heroes

In this resource, the term 'Saint(s)' is understood as applying properly to each disciple of Christ, alongside its reference to Christians whose lives exhibit a distinctive grace of God in following Christ. (The term 'Heroes' is used in places such as The Episcopal Church in Cuba, where 'saints' raises cultural difficulties.)

The ninth Lambeth Conference held in 1958 clarified the commemoration of "Saints and Heroes of the Christian Church in the Anglican Communion". Resolution 79 stated:

- In the case of scriptural saints, care should be taken to commemorate men or women in terms that are in strict accord with the facts made known in Holy Scripture.
- In the case of other names, the Calendar should be limited to those whose historical character and devotion are beyond doubt.
- In the choice of new names, economy should be observed and controversial names should not be inserted until they can be seen in the perspective of history.
- The addition of a new name should normally result from a widespread desire expressed in the region concerned over a reasonable period of time.

Responsibility for the perspectives offered in 'Who was …?', and the adaptations made of liturgical resources, is borne by the author. Corrections or clarifications are welcome, especially for Commemorations. Please contact the publisher, Broughton Publications.

Abbreviations

AAPB	*An Australian Prayer Book (1978)*
APBA	*A Prayer Book for Australia (1995)*
BCP	*The Book of Common Prayer (1662)*
d	died

January 1: The Naming and Circumcision of Jesus

The Circumcision of Christ in *BCP*.
The Naming and Circumcision of our Lord Jesus Christ in *AAPB*.

Why was the incarnate Word circumcised and named 'Jesus'?
The naming and circumcision of a boy went together in Israel of old, a linking of particular significance for understanding the life and ministry of the Lord Jesus Christ.

In biblical times a person's name said a lot about his/her character. So *Isaac* meant 'laughing boy', *Sarai* meant 'princess', and *Jonathan* and *Elnathan* meant 'gift of God'. A change of name had considerable significance: thus *Jacob* meaning 'trickster' became *Israel* meaning 'God-strengthened' and *Simon* became *Peter* meaning 'rock'.

Circumcision was the way by which a male infant, or a man joining Israel, was marked as belonging to the covenant that the Lord established with Abraham (Genesis 17:9–14;). For a boy it was also when they received their name (cf Genesis 21:3–4). *Jesus* — the Greek transliteration of the Hebrew *Joshua* — means 'rescuer, saviour', marking him as one through whom God's people would be saved from their sins (so Matthew 1:21).

Circumcision was a bodily sign that men of God rejected the phallic-centred, fertility-focused ways of life that predominated in the wider world. All Israel was called to 'circumcise the foreskin of your hearts' (Deuteronomy 10:16; Jeremiah 4:4), to live in accordance with the spirit of God's law. This law provided that each male born into Israel would be circumcised on the eighth day (Leviticus 12:3) — a date which hinted at the boy beginning to take part in God's new creation (cf Exodus 22:18–19; Leviticus 14:10, 23; 22:27).

Jesus was named and circumcised on the eighth day (Luke 2:21), thus marking him as a member of Israel, a Jewish male. Interestingly, his circumcision is the only direct evidence in the New Testament that he was male: apart from Ephesians 4:13 (*aner*, of the ascended Christ) he is elsewhere always referred to as 'human' (*anthropos*), most notably in the phrase 'son of *anthropos*'.

A major question faced by the early Church was what to require of uncircumcised men — Gentiles — who responded to the Gospel. Despite the teaching of Genesis, the first Church Council, held in Jerusalem around 49AD, decided that this was not necessary, provided that such converts behaved in ways that did not breach Christian solidarity (Acts 15:1–29).

The apostle Paul in particular argued that requiring anything beyond faith in Christ — itself the gift of the Holy Spirit — contradicted the gospel of God's free grace (cf Galatians 2–3). Christ's ultimate 'circumcision' was his bloody death, which gained forgiveness for all — Jew or Gentile, slave or free, male and female (Galatians 3:28). Further, the abolition of the requirement of circumcision not only allowed Gentiles to enter God's people directly, but also removed any barriers to women being in Christ together with men. Its spiritual significance remains, however: as Christ taught," it is from the heart that all evils come" (Mark 7:21), so that believers need to continually cut off all ungodly thoughts and set their minds on what is true, good and worthwhile (Philippians 4:8).

Christ's obedience saw his ministry transcend the cross, being raised by God to be the first fruits of the new creation, receiving the divine, unknowable Name (cf Exodus 3:13–17), marking him as Lord of all. As Paul wrote to the Philippians (2:9–11):

Therefore God also highly exalted him and gave him the name that is above every name, so that at the name of Jesus every knee should bend, in heaven and on earth and under the earth, and every tongue should confess that Jesus Christ is Lord, to the glory of God the Father.

This is the Name through whom we pray (John 14:13–14; 15:16; 16:23–26) and have eternal life (John 1:12; 20:31), the Name in which the apostles healed and preached (Acts 3:1–15).

'The Naming and Circumcision of Jesus' not only marks his entry into God's people, but points to his opening the new creation to all believers through his atoning death — his 'circumcision' — for the sins of the whole world, from which God raised him to be Lord.

Resources for liturgical use

Service introduction
Christian faith looks to the blood of Jesus for healing — blood first shed when he was circumcised on the first day of his second week and named Jesus, that is, 'saviour'. This is the Name through whom we pray, have eternal life, the Name in which the apostles healed and preached.

Sentences
God spoke of old by the prophets, but in these last days has spoken to us by a Son.

Hebrews 1:1–2

The angel said to Joseph, "The child conceived in Mary is from the Holy Spirit. She will bear a son, and you are to name him Jesus, for he will save his people from their sins."

Matthew 1:20–21

Prayer of the day
God our Father,
you gave to your incarnate Son the name of Jesus
to be a sign of our salvation.
May every tongue confess
that he, who for our sake became obedient to the law,
is both Lord and Christ,
to your eternal glory;
for he now lives and reigns with you and the Holy Spirit,
one God, for ever and ever. **Amen.**

or

Christ our brother,
in you there is neither Jew nor Gentile,
neither male nor female,
yet you received the mark of the covenant,
and took upon yourself
the precious burden of the law.
May we so accept in our bodies
our own particular struggle and promise,
that we also may break down barriers,
in your name. **Amen.**

Readings

Year One (daily cycle)

    Morning Prayer: Psalm 113
                                    Genesis 17:1–13
                                    Colossians 3:12–17

    Evening Prayer: Psalm 113
                                    Exodus 3:13–17
                                    Colossians 2:8–15

Year Two (daily cycle)

    Morning Prayer: Psalm 115
                                    Deuteronomy 30:6–20
                                    Acts 3:1–16

    Evening Prayer: Psalm 115
                                    Deuteronomy 10:12–11:1
                                    Romans 10:5–13

Holy Communion: Numbers 6:22–27
                                  Psalm 8
                                  Galatians 4:4–7
                                  Luke 2:15–21

January 1: New Year's Day

Not in *BCP*, *AAPB* or *APBA*.
Readings in *An Australian Lectionary* from 1998.

Beginning the New Year: some background

According to the Old Testament, the great flood subsided on the first day of the first month (Genesis 8:13). A similar allusion to God's saving work comes after the Exodus from Egypt: the Lord tells Moses that the springtime month of Nisan, when Passover is celebrated "shall mark for you the beginning of months" (Exodus 12:2; cf Leviticus 23:5, Numbers 28:16). In temperate climes this corresponds to April in the southern hemisphere or September in the northern hemisphere. The first day of this first month was also when the Tabernacle is recorded as being first set up (Exodus 40:2, 17), when Hezekiah's cleansing of the Temple began (2 Chronicles 29:17), and when Ezra's expedition from Babylon to Jerusalem set out (Ezra 7:9). The day is not set down for a particular festival in the Mosaic law, but in Ezekiel's vision of the new Temple it was the day when the priests would "purify the sanctuary" (Ezekiel 45:18).

The beginning of the year was thus significant in Israel's understanding of history, associated especially with establishment and renewal of the Tabernacle/Temple. The New Testament gospels portray Jesus as the 'new Temple' (cf John 2:19–22; Mark 14:67–69), and the letters speak of the people of God in Christ in 'temple' terms (cf 1 Corinthians 3:16–17, 6:19; Ephesians 2:12; 1 Peter 2:4–9). The Roman calendar set 1 January as the beginning of the year — Janus was the god whose head had two faces, one looking backwards and the other forwards. In the early centuries, Christians were forbidden to participate in Roman new-year festivities, and in the West it has never been marked liturgically (Sinden, *Times & Seasons*). In the Orthodox East, however, New Year is observed on September 1, alluding to the significance of the day in Israel's calendar. The Annunciation to Mary on 25 March, near the northern–hemisphere spring equinox, was kept as new year's day in the West — the beginning of the new creation — until the eighteenth calendar reforms, when 1 January marked the beginning of the civil year.

John Wesley, desiring both to affirm the significance of the Christmas season, and to distract working men from the attractions of drink, instituted a Covenant Service for the 'people called Methodist', held on the first Sunday of the civil year. In this a congregation solemnly renewed its covenant with God, individuals offering themselves to be open to whatever God may call them. Contemporary forms of this are found in the service books of the Church of South India and the Uniting Church in Australia (*Uniting in Worship*).

In the 19th century, many parish churches began to offer a 'Watchnight service', typically a form of Evening Prayer with a sermon reflecting on the year past, and prayers of dedication and commitment similar to the Covenant Service.

Resources for liturgical use

Service introduction
Israel of old marked the new year in early spring, near Passover. The first day of the first month saw the Tabernacle set up and the Temple cleansed. Christians kept March 25, the northern hemisphere spring equinox, as marking the eternal Word's entry into our human time. This day was observed as New Year's Day until the 18th century, when January 1, as in the ancient Roman calendar, began the year.

Following John Wesley's example, we commit ourselves to serve God in the year ahead.

Sentence

I saw a new heaven and a new earth, and the holy city, the new Jerusalem, coming down out of heaven from God, prepared as a bride adorned for her husband. And the one seated on the throne said, "See, I am making all things new".

Revelation 21:1–2,5

Prayers of the day

(Adapted from Sinden, *Times & Seasons*)
God of all the ages,
your servants have come to the beginning of another year.
Pardon us for the wrongdoings of the past,
and graciously abide with and guide us all our days;
through Jesus Christ our Lord. **Amen.**

Almighty God,
you are the beginning and goal of all creation.
Give us grace to grow in gratitude and holiness,
sufficient prosperity to sustain us,
generosity in sharing the resources of creation,
and wisdom in facing the challenges of the year ahead.
We ask this through our Lord, Jesus Christ,
in whom all things are made new. **Amen.**

Readings

Ecclesiastes 3:1–13 *or* Genesis 8:13–17
Psalm 46 *or* Psalm 62
James 3:13–18 *or* 2 Corinthians 5:16–21
Luke 12:35–40

January 2: Eliza Hassall, pioneer of missionary training and of CMS (d. 1917)

New in *APBA* — description changed, General Synod 2001.

Who was Eliza Hassall?

Eliza Marsden Hassall was born in 1834 at Cobbity, NSW to the Revd Thomas Hassall and his wife Ann, daughter of the Revd Samuel Marsden. Her aunt, Eliza Cordelia Hassall, was married to the Revd William Walker, Wesleyan missionary to the Aborigines.

Eliza Marsden Hassall did not marry, but chose instead to help her father and eldest brother, the Revd James Hassall, in their ministries — the Hassall/Marsden family was a significant clerical community in the developing colony. By 1855 Eliza had become involved in the British and Foreign Bible Society.

Following Thomas' death in 1868, Eliza moved with her mother to Parramatta: she once told her sister-in-law "the lesson affliction is sent to teach us is to be more sympathetic and forgiving to others". In July 1880 Eliza helped form the NSW branch of the *Young* People's Scripture Union, later being its secretary. After the death of her mother in 1885, Eliza helped form the Church Missionary Association of NSW (later CMS).

At the request of the CMA, in 1893 she established the Marsden Training Home for Women Missionaries at her new home, Cluden, and engaged in recruiting new missionaries — the first was her niece Amy Isabel Oxley, who became a missionary to China in 1896. Marsden House proved to be a success, and soon expanded. After an

1899 missionary exhibition, Eliza was made an honorary life member of CMS.

Eliza retired from Marsden House in 1903: by then three of every four Australian overseas missionaries were women whom Eliza had helped recruit and train. The Deaconess Institute at Newtown later took control of Marsden House and continued its work. Eliza died on 26 December 1917 and was buried in the churchyard of St Paul's Church, Cobbitty.

Sources include Ruth Teale, 'Eliza Marsden Hassall' entry, *ADB* and Mary Salmon, Obituary, *Sydney Morning Herald*, 9 January 1918 (online at Obituaries Australia).

Resources for liturgical use

Service introduction
Eliza Hassall, granddaughter of the Revd Samuel Marsden, ministered in the latter half of the 19th century. Choosing not to marry, she worked with her father and brother, both Anglican clergymen, in a range of Christian enterprises, including *Scripture Union*. She is particularly remembered for her pioneering of missionary training for CMS.

Sentence
She who believes in me, even though she dies, will live, and everyone who lives and believes in me will never die.

John 11:25–26

Prayer of the day
(Adapted from 'For a Theologian or Teacher' in *APBA*)
God of all wisdom,
you gave to your servant Eliza Hassall special gifts of grace
to prepare those who would bring the gospel to many lands.
Grant that, enlightened by her example,
we may be equipped by your Holy Spirit
to commend Jesus Christ in our words and deeds,
in whose name we pray. **Amen.**

Readings
Act 9:35–42
Psalm 133
2 Timothy 2:1–13
Luke 8:1–3; 10:1–7

January 6: The Epiphany of our Lord (or the previous Sunday)

The Epiphany, or the Manifestation of Christ to the Gentiles in *BCP* and *AAPB*. *APBA* provides that the feast may be kept on the Sunday preceding 6 January.

What does *epiphany* mean?
Epiphany comes from the Greek *epiphaneo*, literally meaning 'shine out', and so 'manifestation' (as in *BCP*), 'showing forth' or 'revelation'.

Epiphany as a feast

Epiphany as a Christian festival would seem to originate in the Eastern tradition of celebrating the incarnation on 6 January. The West marked this on 25 December, so the 12 days from then until Epiphany became 'the twelve days of Christmas'.

The event associated with Epiphany in the West is the coming of the Magi — the 'wise men from the East' — bringing their three offerings to pay homage to the newborn Christ-child (Matthew 2:1–12). In the East the baptism of Jesus is associated with Epiphany (marked in *APBA* on the Sunday after Epiphany). In either case, the emphasis falls on celebrating the universal reach and significance of God's revelation in Christ.

Epiphany as a season
The relation between Epiphany and Lent in *BCP* is to work backwards from Lent: successive Sundays before Ash Wednesday are Quinquagesima, Sexagesima and Septuagesima, that is, 50, 60 and 70 days before Easter respectively. Epiphany 2 marks the Wedding in

Cana, but the other Sundays after Epiphany (if needed) are regarded as 'ordinary time' rather than marking Epiphany as a season.

In *APBA*, following the *Revised Common Lectionary*, a season of Epiphany is indicated, concluded with the Transfiguration marked as its Last Sunday (*APBA* p. 544), with a First Evensong provided. Epiphany's Sunday gospels thus disclose the public significance of the life and ministry of Jesus as the Christ: Baptism (Epiphany 1); Lamb of God/Nathanael/wedding at Cana (Epiphany 2); call of the Twelve/ Nazareth sermon/initial teaching (Epiphany 3–5) and Transfiguration (Last Sunday). Depending on the date of Easter, other Epiphany Sundays may fall after Pentecost (as the dates noted in *APBA* for each explain): the readings for these follow those for 'ordinary time'.

Epiphany — both as a feast and as a season — is closely associated with the motif of Light. This is reflected in the Sentences and Prayers set out in APBA. The liturgical colour implied is thus white rather than green, the colour traditionally associated with Sundays after Epiphany in BCP.

Resources for liturgical use

Sentence
Arise, shine, for your light has come, and the glory of the Lord has risen upon you.

Isaiah 60:1

The wise men saw the child Jesus with Mary his mother; and they knelt down and worshipped him.

Matthew 2:11

Prayer of the week
O God, dwelling in unapproachable Light,
by the leading of a star you manifested your only-begotten Son to the Gentiles.
Mercifully grant that we, who know you now by faith,
may after this life be led to the vision of your glorious Godhead;
through Jesus Christ our Light and Lord. **Amen.**

Prayers of the day
Lord God of the nations,
we have seen the star of your glory rising in splendour:
may the brightness of your incarnate Word
    pierce the night that covers the earth,
        signal the dawn of justice and peace, and
        beckon all nations to walk as one in your light.
We ask this through Jesus Christ, your Word made flesh,
who lives and reigns with you and the Holy Spirit,
in the splendour of eternal light,
one God for ever and ever. **Amen.**

Eternal God,
by a star you led the Magi to the worship of your Son.
Guide the nations of the earth by your light,
that the whole world may see your glory;
through Jesus Christ our Lord. **Amen.**

Everlasting God,
you brought the nations to your light,
and kings to the brightness of your rising.
Fill the world with your glory,
and show yourself to all the nations,
through him who is the true light and the bright morning star,
Jesus Christ your Son, our Lord. **Amen.**

Readings

First Evensong: Psalm 19
                           2 Samuel 22.47–51
                           Romans 15:8–21
Morning Prayer: Psalm 87
                           Numbers 24:12–17a
                           Ephesians 4:1–16
Evening Prayer: Psalm 104:11–25
                           Exodus 34:5–8
                           Matthew 12:14–23
Holy Communion: Isaiah 60:1–6
                           Psalm 72:1–7, 10–14
                           Ephesians 3:1–12
                           Matthew 2:1–12

January 26: Australia Day

AAPB. APBA includes Prayers and a Proper Preface for Australia.

Australia Day: what does it mean for Christian people?
On 26 January 1788 Governor Arthur Phillip raised the flag of Great Britain in Port Jackson, claiming sovereignty over New Holland, and establishing the penal colony of New South Wales. (The First Fleet had arrived a week earlier, but found Botany Bay unsuitable for settlement.)

In 1808 emancipated convicts celebrated 26 January in honour of the first officer ashore, Major George Johnson (who arrested Governor Bligh the next day). The day was first marked officially in 1818, as Foundation Day, to commemorate the beginning of the NSW colony. As other colonies were established, each kept its own day, with varied names. By 1888, the centenary year of European arrival, most capital cities celebrated 26 January as Anniversary Day: by 1935 all states kept it as Australia Day. From 1946 the Monday following was kept as a national public holiday: since 1994 it is observed on the day itself.

The choice of 26 January as Australia Day has been a matter of debate for many years. In 1938, its sesquicentenary, indigenous Australians marked it as the Day of Mourning, in view of the drastic effect on their lives, culture and society of the establishment of a British penal colony. The 1988 bicentenary saw 26 January marked as Invasion Day in Sydney, and it is now widely known as Survival Day.

Christian observance on the day will reflect its ambiguous history and character. Churches may offer thanksgiving to God for the gifts this land offers, and the privilege of living here. Many will join in local celebrations, and welcome those who take up citizenship on this date. But Christian people cannot avoid facing the sustained injustice experienced by indigenous Australians, the harsh treatment meted out to convicts, the struggle of pioneer settlers to survive, the harm wrought by the White Australia policy, the sectarian rivalry between churches, and the nation's misuse of the earth's resources.

These themes are taken up in the Prayer for the Day. Other prayers of relevance to Australia Day in *APBA* include:
- Forms 3 and 4 of Confession on pages 199–201
- Occasional Prayers 6, 7 and 8 on pages 203–4
- Prayers for those in Need on pages 208–210
- A Thanksgiving for Australia on pages 218–219

Sources include Australian Government information.

Resources for liturgical use

Service introduction
Australia Day has an ambiguous character for Christian people. We give thanks to God for the beauty and blessings of this land, and God's providence in the story of this nation. We remember the dispossession of its indigenous people, the mistreatment of minorities, and the sectarianism between churches. Aware of the great privileges we have today, we commit ourselves to do justice, live generously and walk humbly as disciples of Christ.

Sentence
One generation shall praise your works to another, O Lord, and declare your mighty acts. The Lord upholds all those who stumble, and raises up those that are bowed down.

Psalm 145:4,14

Prayer of the day
Bounteous God,
we give thanks for this ancient and beautiful land,
a land of despair and hope,
a land of wealth and abundant harvests,
a land of fire, drought and flood.
We pray that your Spirit may continue to move in this land
and bring forgiveness, reconciliation, and an end to all injustice;
through Jesus Christ our Lord. **Amen.**

Readings
The scripture readings listed in *APBA* invite reflection on the challenges faced by God's people to follow God's ways, whether the circumstances are familiar and comfortable, or distressing and oppressive. The psalms affirm the Lord's goodness to all, especially when God's ways are lived out.

Deuteronomy 8:5–14a *or* Deuteronomy 28:1–9 *or* Jeremiah 29:4–14
Psalm 125 *or* Psalm 145:1–9 *or* Psalm 33:12–21
Hebrews 11:8–16 *or* Romans 13:1–8 *or* 1 Thessalonians 5:12–24
Matthew 5:1–12 *or* Mark 12:13–17 *or* John 8:31–36

February 3: First Anglican Service on Sydney Cove, conducted by Richard Johnson, Sydney 1788

AAPB and *APBA*.

European Australia: Christian beginnings

The Church of England arrived in this land with the First Fleet, mostly in the soldiers and convicts who belonged to this, the established Church in England. Just one clergyman, the 35-year-old Revd Richard Johnston, a man of Evangelical conviction, was on board the fleet's eleven vessels. He was there only because of political pressure from the Eclectic Society, a group of evangelicals, including William Wilberforce and John Newton, interested in missions and prison reform.

On 3 February 1788, 'under some trees', Johnson conducted public worship for the first time in the new colony, using the *Book of Common Prayer*, and preaching on Psalm 116:12. On 17 February he celebrated Holy Communion in the 'markee' of Lieutenant Clark, who resolved "to keep this table as long as I live, for it is the first table that ever the Lord's Supper was eat of in this country".

His 'flock' consisted of soldiers who mostly mocked him, convicts who mostly ignored him, and a few Aborigines, with whom he was unable to make real contact. Johnson supported Phillip's policy of befriending the Aborigines, took a native girl, Abaroo (Boo-ron) into his family, gave his daughter an Aboriginal name Milbah (b. 1790), and once remained as a hostage while Bennelong visited the Governor.

Johnson faced a nigh-impossible task. He was required to conduct services, keep watch on public morality, oversee schoolmasters and act as magistrate. The authorities saw him as useful for keeping order among the convicts — but refused to help with a building. He worked hard for twelve years, taking services, visiting, baptising, marrying and burying while having to tend his own farm — his main solace from the pressures of life.

When Phillip was succeeded by Lieutenant Governor Francis Grose in 1792, Johnson's time of troubles began. The next year, Johnson, despairing of getting a church built by the government, irritated Grose by putting up a wattle and daub chapel at his own expense — a cost of £67 12s 11½d — only to see it later burnt down. Governor Hunter (1794–96) was more sympathetic, recompensing Johnson for the cost of the chapel.

Johnson supervised the colony's schools, and helped establish an orphan's institution, but was worn out and, after applying for sick leave in 1798, returned to England (with Hunter) in 1800. He died on 13 March 1827.

Sources include Ken Cable, 'Richard Johnson' entry, *ADB*.

Commemorations
The Richard Johnson Anglican School, Oakhurst NSW (Diocese of Sydney).

Richard Johnson Square, corner of Hunter and Bligh Streets, Sydney: the location of the first church building erected in this land.

Resources for liturgical use

Service introduction
The maker and sustainer of all things was present in this land from its earliest beginnings. The first public act of Christian worship took

place on this day in 1788. The Revd Richard Johnson led the service of Morning Prayer in Sydney Cove, preaching on Psalm 116:12. Ever since, not a Sunday has passed in this land without the word of the Lord being heard, and praise and prayer being offered to God in response.

Sentence

What shall I return to the Lord for all his bounty to me? I will lift up the cup of salvation and call on the name of the Lord.

Psalm 116:12–13

Prayer of the day

Everlasting God,
your messengers have carried the good news of Christ
to the ends of the earth.
Grant that we who commemorate
the builders of your Church in this land,
may know the truth of the gospel in our hearts
and build well on the foundations they have laid;
through Jesus Christ our Lord. **Amen.**

Readings

Isaiah 61:8–11
Psalm 116:11–18
Philippians 4:4–8
John 6:25–35

February 20: William Grant Broughton, first bishop of Australia (d. 1853)

New in *APBA*.

Who was Bishop Broughton?

William Grant Broughton was well-educated, well-experienced in church life, and well connected — his appointment as Archdeacon of New South Wales was assisted by the Duke of Wellington. A 'High Churchman', that is, having a high view of the Church in relation to the State. Broughton's aim was to finish what his predecessor, Scott, had sought to do — establish structures for the church in its own right, especially regarding schooling. He was partly lame, using a walking stick, but that did not get in the way of prodigious work.

The chaplaincy system, by then in place for 50 years, saw clergy paid by and accountable to civil rather than church authorities. If the colonial Church was to have its own life, money and manpower must come from England — little support could be found locally. With new colonies forming (Tasmania, Port Macquarie and Brisbane), the need increased, but, despite Broughton's proposals to the government, support failed to materialise. So, having arrived in 1829, he returned to England five years later to raise funds and find clergy.

When came back to Sydney in 1836, it was as the first (and only) Bishop of Australia, though (despite strong objections from Broughton) James Polding had arrived as Roman Catholic Archbishop of Australia the year before. (Polding was the first officially English-recognised RC bishop since the Reformation, made possible by the

1829 *Catholic Emancipation Act*.) Further, the Presbyterian John Dunmore Lang was in a position of influence in the colony.

A 'mixed church' population resided in NSW, with three churches of established ethos (England, Scotland and Ireland) living side by side, an unprecedented situation. There was the prospect of sectarian rivalry, and a critical lack of schooling, despite the churches' varied efforts. Broughton could tolerate the presence of other churches, but believed strongly that only the official Church, established in England, should receive official recognition and support. The *Church Act* of 1836 gave financial support to all three major Churches — the Methodists were included later — but ended any special relationship of the Church of England with the colonial government.

As the colony moved towards some self-government, the Church of England in NSW faced the question of its relationship to England. This issue, exacerbated by the formation of the USA in 1778, faced all of England's colonies: after decades of debate, in 1838 the English Parliament passed *The Colonial Church Act*. In 1842, Tasmania became a diocese, with Francis Nixon as bishop. In 1847 bishops were consecrated for Cape Town, and three dioceses formed from the Diocese of Australia:

- Melbourne (the present Victoria, with Charles Perry as bishop)
- Newcastle (the Hunter to Brisbane, with William Tyrrell as bishop)
- Adelaide (everything west of NSW, with Augustus Short as bishop)

Short and Nixon were High Churchmen, Broughton and Tyrrell (and Selwyn of New Zealand) had been influenced by the Tractarian Movement, and Perry was an Evangelical Churchman. The Diocese of Sydney covered what remained, with Broughton as its bishop, as well as Metropolitan of Australia. But he led a church with no formal state links, and no means of self-government.

In New Zealand, Selwyn had called two synods (of clergy only) in 1844 and 1847. This idea appealed to Broughton so in 1850 he called the six Australasian bishops to an historic month-long conference in Sydney. Considerable interest was taken from overseas since it was not then constitutionally possible for the English bishops to meet together. Could these new colonial bishops offer guidance to the mother church?

Amongst other decisions, two stand out:
- A system of diocesan and provincial synods, of bishop, clergy and laity, should be set up to govern the church: this began in Melbourne and Newcastle in 1854.
- The *Australian Board of Missions* was launched as a 'south-west Pacific mission', with £1000 subscribed to buy a vessel for Selwyn's voyages to Melanesia, and for local Aboriginal work.

Broughton faced considerable difficulties in implementing the Conference decision about synods in NSW, however. Many Sydney clergy continued to embrace the 'chaplaincy' tradition of independence, taking a different stance to Sydney laity. Newcastle wanted the Province rather than the diocese to be the base for church authority.

So Broughton, after 16 years away from England, took a 'most calamitous passage' back in 1852 via South America, on a ship riddled with yellow fever. There he met several other colonial bishops and shared with them his vision for a worldwide union of dioceses in communion with Canterbury. But bronchitis took him in a fortnight, and he was buried in Canterbury Cathedral — a major loss to the churches of the Australian colonies, and what would become the Anglican Communion.

Commemorations

Broughton Books.

Broughton Publications (the national Anglican publisher).

Broughton Hall (*Benetas*), Canterbury, Victoria.

Broughton Anglican College, Menangle Park, NSW.

Resources for liturgical use

Service introduction
William Grant Broughton was the pioneer in seeing the Anglican Church in this land given shape and substance. As the first and only Bishop of Australia, he was called to see the wider picture of God's work. He took the initiative to see new dioceses set up, synodical government introduced, and the Australian Board of Missions formed.

Sentence
You are citizens with the saints and members of the household of God, built upon the foundation of the apostles and prophets, with Christ Jesus himself as the cornerstone.

Ephesians 2:19–20

Prayer of the day
(Adapted from 'For a Bishop' and 'For a Pastor' in *APBA*)
O God, our heavenly Father,
You raised up your faithful servant William Grant Broughton
to be a bishop in your Church,
to feed your flock in this land, and
to be a pioneer of synodical government.
Give abundantly to all bishops,
and especially the Primate of the Anglican Church of Australia,
grace to minister in your household
as true servants of Christ
and stewards of your holy mysteries;
through Jesus Christ our Lord. **Amen.**

or

(Adapted from Gilbert Sinden, *Times & Season*)
God of mercy,
you gave our forebears the light of faith
through the ministry of the pioneer Christians in this land.
Help us who have entered into their labours
to grow in the love and knowledge of your Son,
our Lord Jesus Christ,
in whose name we pray. **Amen.**

Readings
Acts 20:28–36
Psalm 127
2 Corinthians 5:14–20
John 21:15–17

March 9: Sister Emma SSA, superior of the Society of the Sacred Advent, Queensland (d. 1939)

New in *APBA*.

Who was Sister Emma?

Emma Crawford came from Kent to Queensland to join the Society of the Sacred Advent (SSA) in September 1896, aged 33. SSA worked among the poor in England, and had accepted Bishop Webber of Brisbane's invitation to manage an orphanage, a home for women and babies and the Eton High School for girls.

Sister Emma, well educated and with teaching experience, was professed on 28 December 1897. She became sister-in-charge of Eton High, opening the way for more Anglican schools in Queensland. As SSA superior from 1905, she helped develop an industrial school for girls in Brisbane, and in 1909 re-founded a Stanthorpe school as St Catherine's, Warwick.

During World War I Sister Emma accepted the invitation of Bishop Feetham of North Queensland (see September 15) to set up boarding schools for country girls in that diocese. St Anne's, Townsville opened in July 1917; St Mary's, Herberton in 1918; and St Gabriel's, Charters Towers in 1921. All Saints' Hostel, Charleville was later acquired to house far-west children attending the local state school. In 1922 Sister Emma accepted responsibility for St Martin's War Memorial Hospital in Brisbane. Her last major Brisbane venture was founding St Aidan's School in Corinda in February 1929. She took SSA to Rockhampton diocese in 1932, managing St Faith's School at Yeppoon.

Sister Emma SSA died of cancer on 9 March 1939. SSA was by then working in three Queensland dioceses, with similar uniforms and badges, high academic standards and trained staff. It never had more than thirty professed sisters: "responses to the call to the life of a sister are still very rare in Australia," Mother Emma noted in 1906.

Bishop Feetham described Sister Emma SSA as "the principal benefactress" of his diocese. Her ministry played a significant part in moderating the materialism of many aspects of Queensland life. A society contemporary described her as "every inch a lady who could be icy if displeased, but always remained calm, even under great stress".

Sources include Helen Gregory, 'Emma Crawford' entry, *ADB*.

Resources for liturgical use

Service introduction
Sister Emma — born Emma Crawford — was a pioneer of Christian education in North Queensland in the first third of the 20th century. A member of the Society of the Sacred Advent, the schools she founded continue to play a significant role in the kingdom of God.

Sentence
Jesus taught, "If you continue in my word, you are truly my disciples, and you will know the truth, and the truth will set you free."
John 8:31–32

or

You, Lord, are all that I have; I have promised to keep your word. I have sought your favour with all my heart; be gracious to me according to your promise.
Psalm 119:57–58

Prayers of the day
(Adapted from 'For a Teacher' and 'For a Monastic' in *APBA*)
Almighty God,
you gave your servant Sister Emma special gifts of grace
to manage Christian places of learning for girls,
and teach the truth in Christ Jesus.
Grant that, receiving the heritage of her ministry,
young women may know you, the one true God,
and live in the freedom of the truth
through Jesus Christ, our Lord. **Amen.**

O God,
your blessed Son became poor
so that we through his poverty might become rich.
Deliver us from inordinate love of this world.
Inspired by the devotion of your servant Sister Emma,
may we serve you with singleness of heart,
and attain to the riches of the age to come,
through Jesus Christ our Lord,
who lives and reigns with you, in the unity of the Holy Spirit,
one God, now and for ever. **Amen.**

Readings
Deuteronomy 6:1–9 *or* Acts 2:42–47a
Psalm 37:31–41 *or* Psalm 119:161–168
1 Corinthians 1:18–25 *or* 2 Corinthians 6:1–10 *or* 2 Timothy 4:1–5
John 17:18–23 *or* Matthew 6:24–33

March 19: Joseph, husband of the Blessed Virgin Mary

Not in *BCP*. Lesser Festival in *AAPB*. Festival in *APBA*.

Joseph: the stepfather of Jesus

Joseph first appears in the New Testament as the final descendant in the line of Abraham and David, "the husband of Mary, of whom Jesus was born" (Matthew 1:17) — the concluding name in a trio of fourteen generations. He held this position of honour because, responding to God's word through an angel, Joseph took Mary in wedlock though she was carrying a child not his (Matthew 1:18–25). In the following chapter, again prompted by an angel, Joseph takes Mary and the infant to Egypt, out of danger from Herod; when the danger had passed, he settled them in Nazareth, fulfilling another prophecy (Matthew 2:13–23). Joseph comes across as a dignified father figure, largely in the background: when the Magi come, "they saw the child with Mary his mother" — Joseph is not mentioned.

Luke names Joseph as Mary's fiancé (Luke 1:27) and as taking her from Nazareth to Bethlehem, where the child is born, due to his Davidic lineage (Luke 2:4; cf 3:32, 4:22). Joseph is more prominent in Luke than in Matthew: when the shepherds arrive to honour Jesus, Luke says, "they found Mary *and Joseph* and the child" (2:16). Further, Luke notes that "his father and mother" (2:33) were present at Jesus' circumcision and during the family's visit to the Temple a dozen years later (2:41–51), implying Joseph's presence for those years. Beyond that time he disappears from the gospel narratives — was Mary left as a 'single mother' for much of Jesus' life?

Joseph is scarcely mentioned elsewhere in the New Testament. Matthew refers to Jesus once as "the carpenter's son" (13:55), a term which applies to any artisan: since stone is much more common than wood in the buildings of the day, Joseph may have been a stonemason. The only reference to him in John's gospel comes when others note that Jesus was "son of Joseph": Philip to Nathanael (John 1:45) and the crowd at Nazareth (John 6:42). The Acts of the Apostles is silent about Joseph, as are the letters.

This scriptural reticence about Joseph is probably why he does not appear in the Calendar of the *Book of Common Prayer* (1662).

Resources for liturgical use

Service introduction
When God called Joseph to be father to a child not his, his notions of what was right and honourable were turned on their head. In his response, Joseph showed practical wisdom, compassionate care and personal humility. He was content to stay out of the limelight so that Jesus might grow into fulfilling the will of God, as an obedient son.

Sentence
I have calmed and quieted my soul like a weaned child with its mother. O Israel, hope in the Lord, from this time on and for evermore.
Psalm 131:2–3

Prayer of the day

O God,
who from the line of your servant David
raised up the carpenter Joseph
to be the guardian of your incarnate Son
and the husband of Mary his virgin mother:
give us grace to follow Joseph's integrity of life
and his obedience to your commands;
through Jesus Christ our Lord,
who lives and reigns with you and the Holy Spirit,
one God, for ever and ever. **Amen.**

Readings

Morning Prayer:	Psalm 1
	Joel 2:27–32 *or* Genesis 49:22–26
	Ephesians 6:1–4
Evening Prayer:	Psalm 92 *or* 101
	Hosea 11
	Matthew 2:13–23
Holy Communion:	2 Samuel 7:4–16 *or* Joel 2:27–32
	Psalm 89:19–30 *or* Psalm 1
	Romans 4:13–22 *or* Ephesians 6:1–4
	Matthew 1:18–25

April 6: Frederic Barker, bishop and pioneer of Moore Theological College and the General Synod (d. 1882)

New in *APBA*.

Who was Bishop Barker?

Frederic Barker, born in 1808, as a young man came under Charles Simeon's influence at Cambridge, leading to his holding lifelong evangelical convictions. He was ordained priest in 1832 by Bishop Sumner, whose evangelical stance remained Barker's ideal. Jane Sophia Harden, whom he married in 1840, helped him develop intellectually and artistically — her father was a friend of Wordsworth. After 19 years of fruitful parish ministry in Liverpool, where he opposed Roman Catholicism, health issues saw him move to a village church in 1854. But he soon received nomination to Sydney, vacant for over a year after Bishop Broughton's death (see February 20). Barker was consecrated on St Andrew's Day, 30 November 1854, and enthroned in St Andrew's (temporary) Cathedral on 31 May 1855 as Bishop of Sydney and Metropolitan of Australia.

Being nearly two metres tall and teetotal, the tallest beer glass in Sydney hotels was for some years known as a 'Bishop Barker'! His own nickname was 'the High Priest', an ironic referral to his 'low church' stance — that is, supporting a close relationship between Church and Crown. Kindly in personal relations, he saw Tractarians as crypto-Roman, and High Churchmen as too formal. He regarded his chief task to be missionary work across the colony, preaching the gospel in a disarming manner. Building a strong body of clergy to grow churches was his major focus. During his 27 years as Bishop of Sydney, the numbers of churches and clergy more than doubled. He recruited many evangelical ministers from England and Ireland, and oversaw the building of Moore Theological College, led by his friend William Hodgson. These recruits and graduates found allies among 'low church' chaplains from earlier times, becoming an influential group in the diocese.

Barker managed money and parish business superbly, and always willing to ride long distances on horseback. By 1859 Bishopscourt was built, work had resumed on the cathedral and the *Church of England Chronicle* was appearing fortnightly. In 1856 Barker set up the Church Society, based on similar ones in England. A network of parish auxiliaries, under central control, raised local funds for church expansion, and helped prepare the laity to participate in church government. The 1850 bishops' meeting had articulated this need, but only in 1866 did the NSW Parliament pass an Act for church property management, leading to the first meeting of the synod of the Diocese of Sydney soon after.

In 1862 state aid for public worship was abolished in NSW. This saw Barker go to England in 1863 for consultations: he gave many addresses on Australia and raised considerable funds for the Australian church. Barker returned to Sydney committed to the formation of a General Synod. When the Australian bishops had gathered in Sydney for the consecration of St Andrew's Cathedral in 1868, he had pressed the need for this upon them. General Synod began in 1872 and, though its powers were limited (as Barker desired), it was a symbol of unity and a means for cooperation between the colonial dioceses. As Metropolitan of Australia, Barker was actively concerned with their development. While in England he had helped create Goulburn diocese (1863), having earlier been concerned with the establishment of Perth (1856) and Brisbane (1859), and later Grafton & Armidale (1866), Bathurst (1869), Ballarat (1875) and North Queensland (1878).

Barker declined an invitation to the 1867 Lambeth Conference, but went to England in 1870 to seek advice on the changing legal standing of the colonial church. An 1871 English Act had allowed services to be shortened, but Barker resisted other liturgical changes. His England visit also made him wary of biblical criticism and new developments in science.

Christian education was of ongoing concern for Barker, through church schools, religious instruction in public schools and Sunday schools. In 1855 a school for clergy daughters was founded by Jane Barker, in 1859 St Paul's College opened in the new University of Sydney (which had excluded Divinity) and 1868 saw The King's School Parramatta successfully reopened. The 1866 *Public Schools Act* placed all state-supported schools under a single Council of Education, though Barker (as often) was able to secure amendments. His Tory conservatism remained unchanged, however, and was probably intensified by his wife Jane's death on 9 March 1876.

Barker returned to England in 1877 and in January 1878 married Mary Jane Woods and attended the second Lambeth Conference. On returning to Sydney, he became embroiled in debate about Sir Henry Parkes' *Public Instruction Act* of 1880. This introduced compulsory schooling and improved the place of religious instruction in state schools, both of which Barker supported. But it also abolished state aid for church schools, against which he was unable to gain sufficient support in his synod or among the clergy.

In December Barker's health failed, and in March 1881 he left for England to recuperate. However he died on 6 April 1882 while wintering in San Remo, Italy; he was buried in his birthplace of Baslow, Derbyshire.

Sources include Ken Cable, 'Frederic Barker' entry, *ADB*.

Commemorations

The Chapter House at St Andrew's Cathedral, Sydney is designated a Bishop Barker memorial.

Barker College, Sydney North Shore, NSW, was named in honour of Bishop Barker by its founder, the Revd Henry Plume.

Resources for liturgical use

Service introduction

Frederic Barker was called to follow in Bishop Broughton's shoes as Bishop of Sydney. Seeking to live the Christian faith according to the Gospel, Barker became well known around the city and surrounds. His sustained support of new dioceses, local churches, Christian education in schools and theological education laid firm foundations for God's work.

Sentence

An obligation is laid on me, and woe to me if I do not proclaim the gospel! I am entrusted with a commission to do so.

1 Corinthians 9:16–17

Prayer of the day
(Adapted from 'For a Bishop' and 'For a Pastor' in *APBA*)
Heavenly Father,
we bless you for your servant Frederic Barker
whom you called to be a bishop in your Church.
We bless you for his concern
to have your truth made known,
your people well governed,
and the gospel extended across this land.
Give grace to all bishops and other pastors,
so that your people may grow
into the fullness of the stature
of our Lord and Saviour Jesus Christ,
in whose name we pray. **Amen.**

Readings
Deuteronomy 1:9–17 *or* Acts 20:28–36
Psalm 133
2 Corinthians 5:14–20
Luke 22:24–30 *or* John 21:15–17

April 8: Georgiana Molloy, pioneer church leader and botanist from Western Australia (d. 1843)

New in *APBA*.

Who was Georgiana Molloy?

Georgiana Molloy (née Kennedy) was born on 23 May 1805 in the north of England. As a young woman, she was inspired by the preacher Edward Irving to a deep Christian commitment, which saw her distanced from her family. On 1 August 1829 she married Captain John Molloy (who had proposed by letter) and the household sailed to the new Western Australian colony.

With two other families they established a new settlement at Augusta (300 km south of Perth, on the tip of WA's south-west peninsula), where Captain Molloy was appointed resident magistrate. Georgiana bore three daughters and a son at Augusta: the eldest daughter died at birth and the son drowned at 19 months. Augusta was difficult country, and settlers began to leave. In 1839 the Molloys moved to the Vasse River (100 km north) where Fair Lawn homestead was built, and two more daughters were born. Until this move the Molloys' life was hard: as magistrate, Captain Molloy was often away from home and Georgiana's diary shows she wished to return to England.

Georgiana had a keen eye for indigenous flowers, which she pressed and mounted. In 1836 Captain James Mangles wrote from England, asking her to send seeds of native plants: his unexpected letter inspired in Georgiana a passion for botany. Over the next few years she spent time collecting and describing seeds, making use of local Aborigines' knowledge of plants. Her shipments included written descriptions of the plants, and albums of pressed flowers: the seeds were distributed to English botanical gardens. Other collectors' parcels were poorly prepared and often failed to germinate in England, but hers were clearly identified and carefully packed, arriving in fresh condition. Her botanical work was listed in significant publications, including George Bentham's *Flora Australiensis* series (London, 1863–78), and botanists came from the Continent to visit her. Some of her albums of pressed flowers are kept at the Herbariums at Kew and the University of Cambridge.

Alongside botanical work and household responsibilities, Georgiana played a significant part in commencing and sustaining local congregations in pioneer settlements south of Perth. The Molloy's eldest daughter, Sabina, married Matthew Blagden Hale, who would become the first Anglican Bishop of Perth.

Each of her pregnancies led to periods of ill health: three months after her sixth daughter was born she died at Fair Lawn, just 37 years of age, on 8 April 1843. Horticulturist George Hailes wrote to Captain Mangles after learning of Georgiana's death: "Not one in ten thousand who go out into distant lands has done what she did for the Gardens of her Native Country."

Sources include Alexandra Hasluck, 'Georgiana Molloy' entry, *ADB*.

Commemorations
The shrub *Boronia molloyae*, (Australian Christmas tree), which appears on the crest of the Georgiana Molloy Anglican School in Busselton, WA, was named in her honour.

Augusta, WA features the Georgiana Motel, and Molloy Island is nearby.

Georgiana: Woman of Flowers, by Libby Hathorn (Hachette, 2008) is a young adult novel based on her life.

Resources for liturgical use

Service introduction
Georgiana Molloy embodied God's concern for the natural world, beyond the church and the human race. While facing the difficulties of pioneer life for women in Western Australia, Georgiana gave herself both to careful botanical research, and to sustained initiatives in church planting.

Sentence
"Consider the lilies of the field, how they grow; they neither toil nor spin. Yet I tell you," said the Lord Jesus, "even Solomon in all his glory was not clothed like one of these."

Matthew 6:28

Prayer of the day
(Adapted from 'For a Saint' in *APBA*)
Faithful God,
you have surrounded us with a great cloud of witnesses.
By your grace, your servant Georgiana Molloy
bore the cost of bringing children to birth,
and became a shining light in exploring the wonders of botany.
Grant that we, encouraged by her example,
may persevere in running the race set before us.
Like her, may we be steadfast when commitment is costly,
with our eyes open to the wonders of your creation,
through Jesus Christ, the pioneer and perfector of our faith. **Amen.**

Readings
Proverbs 31:10–31
Psalm 15
Hebrews 11:32–12:2
John 11:17–44

April 11: George Augustus Selwyn, first missionary bishop of New Zealand (d. 1878)

AAPB and *APBA*.

Who was Bishop Selwyn?

Selwyn went to school with John Henry Newman, and at Eton came to know William Ewart Gladstone. At Cambridge he was a crew-member in the first Oxford–Cambridge Henley-on-Thames boat race in 1829. After graduating in 1831 he tutored at Eton before being ordained deacon in 1883 and priest in 1834 — believing that "among the professions, this will in future be the most laborious and the least lucrative" (cited in Limbrick). He was elected a Fellow of St John's College, Cambridge in 1833, tutoring until 1840 alongside curacy at Windsor, where "his energetic ministry drew attention, including that of Prince Albert". Selwyn married Sarah Harriet Richardson on 25 June 1839: their son John rowed for Cambridge, and would later become Bishop of Melanesia.

In 1841 the Bishop of London offered the new post of Bishop of New Zealand to Selwyn (whose brother William had declined it). Consecrated bishop on 17 October 1841, he left for his new diocese on 26 December with a party numbering two dozen, as well as various animals and four hives of bees. On the voyage, Selwyn studied Maori with the help of a Maori boy, and could preach in it when the group reached Sydney in April 1842. Leaving their families to follow later, Selwyn and William Cotton (his chaplain) soon set sail for New Zealand, reaching Auckland on 30 May. "To see the

Bishop handle a boat was almost enough to make a man a Christian", Limbrick reports one sailor having said of Selwyn's maritime skills.

Selwyn set up residence at Waimate, 15 miles inland from where the Church Missionary Society had settled in the Bay of Islands in 1831. On 5 July 1842, just 10 days after arriving, Selwyn set out on a six-month, 2300-mile tour of his diocese, leaving Waimate in the care of his wife Sarah and William Cotton. In 1843, accompanied by Cotton, Selwyn embarked on a second six-month tour, by canoe and walking. Later in 1844, after tensions with CMS, Selwyn moved 160 miles south, where he bought 450 acres near Auckland. In December 1847 Selwyn began voyages to the Pacific Islands, which resulted in the consecration of John Coleridge Patteson (see September 20) as Bishop of Melanesia in 1861.

Selwyn "visited every part of the country," states Limbrick. "His visitation journals record baptisms, confirmations and marriages of whalers, settlers and sawyers, Maori and Pakeha. He taught and preached in both languages, selected church sites, established schools, administered trusts, fostered isolated mission stations and confirmed lonely settlers. His advice was in demand by governors and politicians, Maori elders and teachers."

The Diocese of New Zealand (along with Australia) was one of the early colonial sees organised from England (see February 20). Selwyn, seeing the need for self-government, in 1844 and 1847 held synods of local clergy — acts which raised questions in England — and took part in the 1850 meeting of bishops in Sydney. In 1854 he visited England to have New Zealand subdivided into dioceses, and allowed to manage its own affairs by a General Synod, on the basis of 'voluntary compact'. In 1856 the Dioceses of Auckland and Christchurch formed (the North and South Islands), and an 1857 conference led to a Constitution for the Church of the Province of New Zealand being adopted — seen as Selwyn's most significant legacy. In 1858 Waiapu and Nelson dioceses formed, and in 1859 General Synod met under Selwyn as Primate of New Zealand and Bishop of Auckland.

Meanwhile the New Zealand land wars had interrupted the progress of Christian mission among the Maori. Selwyn was a keen critic of the land acquisition practices of the New Zealand Company. His efforts in Christian ministry to both sides were indefatigable, but he was misunderstood by Englishmen and some Maori. Against settler opinion, Selwyn argued for the education of young Maori, so they might adjust to the new situation "without distinction of persons". In 1847 he set up St John's College, which integrated a theological college, collegiate school, Maori teachers' and boys' schools, an infant school and hospital. However, Limbrick states, "Selwyn's reach exceeded his grasp, for the complex project foundered on financial difficulties, inadequate staff, and settler opposition to equality of race. The college closed in 1853." Today St John's offers theological college for the Province, for which its valuable land forms an endowment.

In 1867 Selwyn visited England for a second time to participate in the first Lambeth Conference. While there he accepted, with much reluctance, the invitation to become Bishop of Lichfield, and was enthroned on 9 January 1868. Some months later he paid a farewell visit to New Zealand, to chair its fourth General Synod. On 20 October, at a farewell communion service, "the final communicant to receive the bread and the wine from the bishop's hands was the venerable Ngati Hao chief Patuone. A public holiday was declared to farewell Selwyn … The streets were decked with bunting; steamers sounded their whistles; naval vessels fired their guns." (Limbrick)

Limbrick writes that Sarah, "known among Maori as 'Mata Pihopa' (Mother Bishop), never wavered in support of her husband, though he was away for long periods … Sarah suffered a good deal from ill health. She found life much more agreeable after her return to England with Selwyn in 1868. She lived a long and contented life at Lichfield until her death in 1907."

Selwyn presided over Lichfield until his death on 11 April 1878, aged 69. "It is said that his last words were in Maori, and that they meant 'It is all light'." (Limbrick)

Sources include Warren E. Limbrick, 'Selwyn, George Augustus', the *Dictionary of New Zealand Biography* and *Te Ara — the Encyclopedia of New Zealand* (online).

Commemorations
Selwyn College, Cambridge, England (1882).

Selwyn College, Otago, New Zealand (1893). Selwyn Houses at The King's School, Auckland and at Wellesley College, Wellington, New Zealand.

Memorial in Lichfield Cathedral.

Resources for liturgical use

Service introduction
George Selwyn left England to be the first Bishop of New Zealand. Learning Maori on the ship that took him there, he became a strong supporter of Maori as well as settler interests. He travelled widely across New Zealand and the Pacific expanding centres of mission. He is especially remembered for enabling the Anglican Province of Aotearoa, New Zealand to live as a self-governing Church.

Sentence

You whom I took from the ends of the earth, and called from its farthest corners:
Do not fear, for I am with you, do not be afraid, for I am your God.
I will strengthen you, I will help you.

Isaiah 41:10–11

Prayer of the day

(Adapted from the Church of the Province of Aotearoa, New Zealand)
Almighty and everlasting God,
we thank you for your servant George Augustus Selwyn,
whom you called to preach the Gospel to the peoples of New Zealand and Melanesia,
and to lay a firm foundation for the growth of your Church in many nations.
Raise up in this and every land,
evangelists and heralds of your kingdom,
that your Church may proclaim the unsearchable riches of our Saviour Jesus Christ,
who lives and reigns with you and the Holy Spirit,
one God, now and for ever. **Amen.**

Readings

Isaiah 55:1–11
Psalms 16, 126
1 Corinthians 3:7–13 *or* Ephesians 2:11–18
Luke 10:1–12 *or* John 4:31–18

April 25: Anzac Day

AAPB. Prayers and Readings added in *APBA*.

Anzac Day: what does it mean for Christian people?
Anzac Day commemorates the landing of Australian and New Zealand troops at Gallipoli, Turkey (then part of the Ottoman Empire) on 25 April 1915. After enduring a determined enemy, difficult living conditions and significant losses, ANZAC forces made a successful withdrawal in December, planned by their leaders. The campaign was a failure, but their military reputation was enhanced, marked by bravery under fire, acceptance of danger, a spirit of 'make-do' and independence, and deep camaraderie. That Anzac Day marks a noble defeat is important for Australian identity, evoking the pioneer tradition of persevering through adversity.

Anzac commemorations began the following year, and have continued since. Two Anglican clergymen shaped its early character. The Revd Albert White initiated a dawn service in Albany, WA, the point of departure for most Australian troops. After the refrain "As the sun rises and goeth down, we will remember them", he led those present in prayer, and 'Last Post' and 'Reveille' were played. In Queensland, Canon David Garland promoted the day as "Australia's All Souls' Day"; he placed Binyon's 'Ode to the Fallen' on the cover of a 1921 service booklet. But the Great War had brought a deep sense of mourning which transcended Australian class and sectarian divisions. Both men were thus conscious that the day held a wide significance, and sought to develop rituals in which those of any faith or none could participate. Thus, in the face of diverse understandings of 'prayer for the dead', the (originally two) minute silence was introduced to allow each person present to pray, or not pray, in accordance with his or her individual beliefs.

Anzac Day services have been sponsored by bodies such as the RSL since 1929, when the day was first observed nationally, and the participation of Christian clergy is generally welcomed. There are dangers involved, not so much of glorifying war, as of confusing ideas about 'sacrifice', notably overly close parallels between the atoning death of Christ and the tragic death of military forces. Soldiers do not go to war looking to die, to 'sacrifice themselves', but rather look to return home safely. Yet the willingness to face danger, becoming disabled or even dying is profoundly praiseworthy.

The ambiguous character of the day remains important, including the linking of the serious services of the morning with the games of the afternoon. Christian churches can make a significant contribution by continuing to point to solidarity in the face of defeat as shaping our national character, rather than the triumphal celebration of our achievements.

Resources for liturgical use

Sentence
"No one has greater love than this," said Jesus, "than to lay down one's life for one's friends."

John 14:13–14

Prayers of the day
[Adapted from *APBA* and from Gilbert Sinden, *Times & Seasons*]
O God, our ruler and guide,
in your hands are the destinies of this and every nation.
We give you thanks for the freedoms we enjoy in this land,
and for those who laid down their lives to defend them.
We pray that we, and all the people of Australia and New Zealand,
gratefully remembering their courage and their sacrifice,
may have grace to live in a spirit of justice, of generosity, and of peace.
through Jesus Christ our Lord. **Amen.**

God of love and liberty,
we bring our thanks today for the peace and security we enjoy.
We remember those who in time of war faithfully served their country.
We pray for their families, and for ourselves,
whose freedom was won at such a cost.
Make us a people zealous for peace,
and hasten the day when nation shall not lift up sword against nation
neither learn war any more.
This we pray in the name of the one who gave his life
for the sake of the world:
Jesus Christ, our Redeemer. **Amen.**

God our Father,
your Son our Lord has taught us
that those who work for peace will be called your children.
Grant wisdom and integrity
to the people of Australia and their leaders,
that harmony and justice may always prevail in our land,
and there may be lasting prosperity and peace
in the world you have made for us to live in.
We ask this through our Lord Jesus Christ. **Amen.**

Readings

Micah 4:1–4 *or* 2 Samuel 22:2–20

Psalm 46 *or* Psalm 51:14–19

Hebrews 10:32–11.1 *or* Romans 5:1–8

John 15:9–17 *or* John 10:1–21

May 27–June 3: Week of Prayer for Reconciliation

New in *APBA*.

What is the 'Week of Prayer for Reconciliation'?
The historic '*Mabo* judgment' was handed down by the Australian High Court on 3 June 1992. This recognised that Eddie Mabo, on behalf of his people, held 'native title' to the lands in the Torres Strait on which they had lived for generations. In effect, their possession of this land — in part sustained by their Anglican identity — had never been removed. The decision gave all Australians a new 'imagining' of the land, setting aside the notion of it being 'terra nullius' — empty prior to European settlement.

The date fell a week after the anniversary of the Referendum, which took place on 27 May 1967, that removed words from the Constitution that (i) excluded government responsibility for the "the aboriginal people in any State", and (ii) excluded Aboriginal people from being counted in the Census. The Referendum, which passed with over 90 per cent voting in its favour, took effect from 10 August 1967. The change was a small step — not until 1995 could indigenous Australians vote in every state — but marked the beginnings of the process of reconciliation.

When the *National Council of Churches in Australia* formed in 1994, its first Forum set up the Week of Prayer for Reconciliation, to run each year from 27 May to 3 June. The week was included in the Calendar of *APBA* (1995), along with 'Coming of the Light' on 1 July, which commemorated the arrival of the Gospel to the Torres Strait.

But there is a longer history behind these commemorations. Despite many failures and misunderstandings, Australian churches have sought to share the Gospel with the indigenous people of this land from the first arrival of Europeans. In 1910, based on their experience of mission work, the *Australian Board of Missions* and the *Church Missionary Society* proposed that each church set aside one Sunday each year to focus on indigenous issues. They proposed the scripture readings set out in the Resources for liturgical use on p. 55.

'Reconciliation' has a wide meaning in the scriptures. It is grounded in the life-giving work of Jesus Christ, whose atoning death was the means of all things being reconciled to God — and calling us to be reconciled to one another (cf Matthew 5:24). As Paul taught,

> In Christ all the fullness of God was pleased to dwell; through Christ God was pleased to reconcile to himself all things, whether on earth or in heaven, by making peace through the blood of his cross.
>
> **Colossians 1:19-20**

> God reconciled us to himself through Christ, and has given us the ministry of reconciliation; that is, in Christ God was reconciling the world to himself, not counting their trespasses against them, and entrusting the message of reconciliation to us. So we are ambassadors for Christ, since God is making his appeal through us: we entreat you on behalf of Christ, be reconciled to God.
>
> **2 Corinthians 5:17-21**

In this land, the mistreatment, misunderstandings and abuse of its indigenous peoples by those who have arrived since 1788 has been called its 'original sin'. It carried over to racist behaviour and attitudes towards 'non-white' immigrants — the 'White Australia' policy, finally dismantled in 1973. Australia's churches long acted toward one another in sectarian ways, rather than seeing each other as fellow citizens of heaven. All these, and other aspects of reconciliation, can be brought to mind in this week, but its particular focus must remain on our 'original sin'.

The week provides opportunities for congregations to engage with those who are 'different' to them. Looking for indigenous stories around where we live is a good place to start — if there are no personal contacts, the local library can often help.

Resources for liturgical use

Service introduction
The Week of Prayer for Reconciliation began in 1994, and runs from 27 May to 3 June each year. It gives opportunity for prayer and action towards reconciliation in the life of this nation, especially between indigenous and immigrant Australians.

The dates are significant. The Mabo decision, which changed our legal system to include native title rights, was handed down by the High Court on 27 May 1992. On 3 June 1967, a Referendum was passed by over 90% to change the Australian Constitution to allow indigenous Australians to be included in the Census — the first small step towards their recognition as full citizens.

Sentence
Jesus said, "When you are offering your gift at the altar, if you remember that your brother or sister has something against you, leave your gift there before the altar and go; first be reconciled to your brother or sister, and then come and offer your gift."

Matthew 5:23-24

Prayers of the day

(*APBA Prayers for Various Occasions* #6, written by Bishop Arthur Malcolm; Prayer of the Day, Australia Day)

Lord God, bring us together as one,
reconciled with you and reconciled with each other.
You made us in your likeness,
    you gave us your Son, Jesus Christ.
    He has given us forgiveness from sin.
Lord God, bring us together as one,
    different in culture, but given new life in Jesus Christ,
    together as your body, your Church, your people.
Lord God, bring us together as one,
    reconciled, healed, forgiven,
    sharing you with others as you have called us to do.
In Jesus Christ, let us be together as one. **Amen.**

Bounteous God,
we give thanks for this ancient and beautiful land,
a land of despair and hope,
a land of wealth and abundant harvests,
a land of fire, drought and flood.
We pray that your Spirit may continue to move in this land
and bring forgiveness, reconciliation, and an end to all injustice;
through Jesus Christ our Lord. **Amen.**

Forms of Confession #3 and #4 may also be appropriate: these require preparation.

Readings:

Psalm 33:12–21 *or* Psalm 125
1 John 4:7–21 *or* 2 Corinthians 5:10–20
Luke 16:19–31

July 1: Coming of the Light, first missionaries to the Torres Strait (1871)

New in *APBA* — Lesser Festival with Prayer and Readings.

What was 'The Coming of the Light'?

'I am the Light of the World.' Thank God for the first missionaries, who on July the first 1871, at Darnley Island, brought the light of Christ to the Torres Strait.

So reads the inscription outside the Anglican Church on Thursday Island. The following year, London Missionary Society pastors arrived at Mer; by 1900, virtually all Murray Islanders professed to be Christians, following Anglican ways.

Torres Strait Islanders come together on 1 July to celebrate 'The Coming of the Light'. More Islanders live in Queensland than on the islands themselves these days, but the day is marked wherever they live. While most Islanders are Anglican, led by Islander clergy, the day is marked by all, of whatever Christian tradition.

On Saturday evening 1 July 1871, the ship carrying the Revd Samuel MacFarlane of the London Missionary Society, together with South Sea Islander evangelists and teachers, anchored at Erub (Darnley Island). Dabad, a local clan elder, defied his tribal law and openly welcomed the party. A tradition existed in the Islands that when white men arrived on a large canoe carrying a sacred object (MacFarlane was holding a Bible), they were to be listened to. Asked by researcher David Salisbury about the day's significance,

Father Elimo Tapin of St Stephen's Anglican Church, Townsville responded:

> For us the celebration of the Coming of the Light is just like celebrating Christmas day. On Christmas day God came to us in the form of a baby and on July 1 God came to the Torres Strait in the form of a book.[1]

Church services and a re-enactment of the landing are central to the day's activities. Hymn singing, feasting and *Ailan dans* ('Island dance' — but contrasted with pre-1871 war dances) strengthen community and family ties.

Torres Strait Islanders' acceptance of Christianity brought changes that profoundly affected every aspect of their lives. It ended inter-island conflict, bringing the Islanders into a wider culture together. Christian ideas were somewhat compatible with Islanders' traditional beliefs, and Anglican leaders allowed tribal cultural elements to continue in worship. Further, Islanders had been grossly exploited in the maritime industry: missionaries provided some protection and assistance in negotiations.

Today Torres Strait Islanders live all over Australia, especially in Queensland, and TSI Anglicans have their own bishop. The Mabo case, handed down on 3 June 1992, led to the recognition of Native Title rights for all indigenous Australians. That date now marks the end of the Week of Prayer for Reconciliation, which opens on 27 May (Census Day 1967).

Sources include the websites of the Anglican Board of Mission — Australia, the Torres Strait Regional Authority, and the Queensland Museum.

---

1 David Salisbury, 'The Coming of the Light. Spirituality in Diaspora.' 7th International Small Islands Conference, Airlie Beach, Whitsundays, Queensland, 12–15 June 2011, accessed from http://sicri-network.org/ISIC7/n.%20ISIC7P%20Salisbury.pdf

Resources for liturgical use

Service introduction
On the first day of July 1871, a ship bearing London Missionary Society personnel arrived on Darnley Island in the Torres Strait, with copies of the Bible. They were received as fulfilling a long-held local tradition, and the gospel of Christ took root quickly. The day has since been marked by all Islanders as 'The Coming of the Light'.

Sentence
Jesus said, "I am the light of the world. Whoever follows me will never walk in darkness but will have the light of life."

John 8:12

Prayer of the day
Almighty God,
you have given to the people of the Islands
of the Torres Strait
the glorious light of the Gospel of Christ.
Mercifully grant that we may always walk
in the light of his love,
and give us the strength and unifying power
of your Holy Spirit to spread that light
and enlarge your kingdom in the hearts of all people.
We ask this through our Lord Jesus Christ, your Son,
who lives and reigns with you and the Holy Spirit,
one God, for ever and ever. **Amen.**

Readings
Isaiah 58:8–11
Psalm 27
2 Corinthians 4:5–6
John 12:35–47

July 13: Sydney James Kirkby, bishop, pioneer of outback ministry and the Bush Church Aid Society (d. 1935)

New in *APBA*.

Who was Bishop SJ Kirkby?

Sydney James Kirkby (known as 'SJ') was born in 1879 in Bendigo, and grew up as a Christian of firm evangelical conviction. He became a Lay Reader at White Hills in 1902; sent by the Bishop of Bendigo to prepare for ordained ministry at Moore College, he blossomed there, being senior student for 1905. He was deaconed on 24 December 1905 and priested a year later, becoming rector of Malmsbury: between ordinations he married Victoria Ethel Godfrey. A vigorous pastor, imbued with a deep scholarly spirituality, in 1911 he returned to Moore as acting principal, gaining a BA from the University of Durham. In 1914 he became rector of St Anne's, Ryde.

As 'soldier settlements' opened after the Great War, the needs of outback Australians were again recognised by Anglicans. A group of evangelical clergy formed the Bush Church Aid Society in 1919, led by the first Bishop of Gippsland, Arthur Pain, and the Revd George Chambers, later the first Bishop of Tangyanika. "Australia for Christ" was its motto, and "we begin where the railway ends" its slogan. Kirkby, believing that evangelicals had a part to play in missions to the outback, became its first Organising Missioner.

Work began in Cobar (Bathurst diocese) in 1920, then Wilcannia and in the Far West Mission in South Australia. Travel was difficult, distances great, drought prevailed, and many traditional 'church' ways were either impossible or irrelevant. Kirkby would never send out a missioner without having travelled the area himself. A 1920 photograph shows him dressed in tie and hat, carrying his swag, as he tramped the Croajingalong forests near Cann River in Gippsland. This visit saw a deaconess and a nurse take up ministry in the area, living in tents and then a paling shed: BCA was open to women workers as well as men.

A strong man and of plain habits, Kirkby 'carried his swag' and faced hardship on his outback tours. Under God, good organisation and modern technology would make BCA effective. Missioners were trained in Sydney and Melbourne and imported from England, and nurses recruited for hospitals and hostels in the far west of NSW and South Australia. From his Sydney base Kirkby ran a steady publicity campaign, editing the BCA journal, *Real Australian*, and writing in 1929 a vivid account of its work, *These Ten Years*.

In 1927 the Revd Len Daniels, a former WWI pilot, became the first 'flying parson': Kirkby enjoyed flying with him, taking photographs to promote BCA's work. BCA also pioneered the use of aircraft for medical use in Australia, commencing the Flying Medical Service from Ceduna: this became part of the Royal Flying Doctor Service in 1968. Distance education was another BCA initiative: its School of the Air was later incorporated into the SA Education Department. At its peak in 1939, the Mail-Bag Sunday School involved 4,500 children helped by 60 voluntary workers. Motor vans were another innovation: workers moved around homesteads — camping — to take services, using a gramophone or baby organ. A 'Women's Mission Van' was questioned by some, but Kirkby believed it was "right and safe" for women to be involved in ministry.

The Stockman's Hall of Fame and Outback Heritage Centre, Longreach, after recognising his Christian ministry, says this of Kirkby as a man:

He understood the outback settlers, their way of looking at things and doing things, and, in turn, was trusted by them. In his zeal for Australia his gifts were developed. He was a keen photographer, making and tinting his own glass slides, a good pianist, pen sketcher, and modest poet. He enjoyed joining in the fun and promoting social activities whether travelling by ship or amongst communities.

In 1932 Kirkby was recalled to diocesan affairs, appointed as bishop coadjutor of Sydney — but within months found himself in charge after Archbishop Wright's death. He applied himself vigorously to the financial and social problems of Sydney, still suffering from the Depression. As bishop coadjutor he was rector of St Philip's Sydney: he sustained a lively ministry there, his weekday lunchtime services drawing large crowds. Presiding over the archbishop's election, he saw Bishop Howard Mowll of West China elected, though many wished that Kirkby had accepted nomination. He continued as assistant to the archbishop and, with more enthusiasm, as minister at St Philip's Sydney. Suffering from chronic nephritis, Bishop Kirkby died on 12 July 1935, and was buried in the grounds of St Philip's. His wife Victoria, two sons and two daughters survived him.

Sources include Ken Cable, 'Sydney James Kirkby' entry, *ADB*; BCA archives; and Stockman's Hall of Fame.

Commemorations
Bishop Kirkby Memorial Hospital, Cook (on the Transcontinental Railway).

Commemorative plaque, St Anne's, Ryde, Sydney.

Resources for liturgical use

Service introduction
Bishop Sydney James Kirkby (known as 'SJ') was the first Missioner of the fledging Bush Church Aid Society. He was a man of energy, pastoral experience and learning: he had taught at Moore College, and is commemorated in the Stockman's' Hall of Fame. Kirkby gave himself to serve the people of the outback, taking initiatives such as the Flying Medical Service, the School of the Air and employing women as well as men in ministry.

Sentence
The love of Christ urges us on, because we are convinced that one has died for all, so that those who live might live no longer for themselves, but for him who died and was raised for them.
2 Corinthians 5:14–15

Prayer of the day
(Adapted from 'For a Missionary' in *APBA*)
God of all the nations,
we thank you for your servant Sydney James Kirkby,
whom you called to bring the gospel
both to the people of outback Australia,
and to the growing city of Sydney.
Raise up in this and every land, we pray,
evangelists and bishops to proclaim your loving reign,
so that the whole world may know
the unsearchable riches of our Saviour Jesus Christ,
in whose name we pray. **Amen.**

The *Bush Church Aid Society* prayer
Lord our God, we pray for all who live in remote parts of Australia.
Thank you for the Bush Church Aid Society:
for its ministry of word and sacrament,
its medical work and support services, and its care for the young.
Encourage workers in loneliness, and refresh them in hardship.
Call many to stand with them in making Christ known,
that your redeeming love might be accepted throughout our land.
This we pray in Jesus' name. **Amen.**

Readings
Isaiah 52:7–10
Psalm 96
2 Corinthians 4:5–15
Luke 10:1–9

August 15: Mary, Mother of our Lord

Not in *BCP* or *AAPB*. Festival in *APBA*, with First Evensong, Introduction to Confession, Proper Preface, Prayer after Communion, and Blessing.

Why celebrate Mary on this day?

Mary, the mother of Jesus, our Lord and Christ, has a distinctive place among God's people. Yet until the inclusion of this day (15 August) in *APBA*, Australian Anglicans had no Festival to celebrate the ministry of Mary in her own right. *BCP* retained five pre-Reformation feasts that relate to her: Presentation (2 February), Annunciation (25 March), Visitation (31 May), her Birth (8 September) and Conception (8 December). But at the time of the Reformation in the Church of England, 15 August was omitted from the calendar, due to its strong links with Marian devotions, which set her alongside Christ.

The gospels bear witness to Mary as the mother of Jesus (Matthew and John especially). Her response to the word of God through Gabriel, "let it be (*fiat*) to me according to your word" (Luke 1:38) is the exemplar of Christian obedience. Mary celebrates God's saving work in song (Luke 1:46–55 — its first word is *Magnificat* in Latin), hears Simeon and Anna's welcome to the Saviour and word of warning (Luke 2:29–38) and "treasured all these things in her heart" (Luke 2:51), reflections no doubt recalled on the day of Pentecost (Acts 1:14). John's gospel never uses her name: she is "the mother of Jesus", directing others to him (John 2:5) and staying with him to death. John initially speaks of Jesus as part of his mother's family

(John 2:1–2), but after his first miracle she is his follower, herself a disciple (John 2:12). Mark emphasises this point, that the true 'family' of Christ are not his earthly relatives: "Whoever does the will of God is my brother and sister" (Mark 3:35).

Mary's distinctive place as 'mother of our Lord' played a key role in the responses made in the early church to false teaching. Against docetism (that Jesus only 'seemed' (*dokeo*) to be human) it was emphasised that he did not just 'pass through' Mary's womb, but was born of her flesh (cf 1 John 4:2). Conversely, when questions were raised about the true deity of Christ, that Jesus was "conceived of the Holy Spirit and born of the Virgin Mary" (Apostles' Creed) was seen as witnessing to his divine origin and identity. Mary was thus confessed as *Theotokos*, 'she who bore God', as the Chalcedonian Definition puts it.[2]

The Church of England shares this patristic heritage, but at the Reformation objected to the 'cult' of Mary, which had gradually developed in the previous centuries. In 1854 the Pope declared as a matter of faith the long tradition, celebrated on 15 August, that Mary had been 'assumed body and soul' into heaven. Anglicans can affirm that Mary, as mother of our Lord, shares the glory of God's kingdom, and has a unique place among God's people. Of all the saints, she is most truly alive in Christ, as *Theotokos* still. But the lack of a scriptural basis for her 'assumption' raises questions, and any idea of her being exalted at the expense of Christ is rejected.

Tragically, sharpening Protestant-Catholic polemics meant that "to be Roman Catholic came to be identified by an emphasis on devotion to Mary"[3], while for many Anglicans she was effectively absent

---

[2] *Theotokos* can be translated as 'mother of God' in English, a rendition commonly misunderstood among Protestants as implying that Mary is mother of the Creator. Anglicans affirm the term's intention, to bear clear witness to the deity of Christ, but 'mother of God' is not used in Anglican formularies.

[3] ARCIC II, *Mary: Grace and Hope in Christ* (London: SPCK / CTS, 2005) section 47. This Agreed Statement faces the questions that have arisen about Mary, including the 1854 and 1950 papal dogmas, and offers fresh ways of understanding and apprehending her ministry.

from their Christian lives. Over the past fifty years these contrasts have significantly lessened. On the Roman Catholic side, the Second Vatican Council (1962–65) taught that Mary must only be seen in relation to Christ and the Church, and Pope Paul VI's 1974 encyclical *Marialis Cultus* gave clear teaching about her ministry. On the Anglican side, the distinctive place of Mary in God's economy of salvation has been appreciated afresh, so that, across the Communion, 15 August has been restored to celebrate the distinctive ministry of Mary in her own right, as 'Mother of our Lord'.

For Anglicans, the most familiar form of 'Marian devotion' is the praying of her song (the *Magnificat*) at Evening Prayer. We use it not only as a hymn from the past, but join in singing it to the praise of God with her, as truly alive in Christ. Mary is thus a 'type', a living symbol of the whole people of God, the body of Christ. This is the focal point of celebrating her feast on this day. As ARCIC II concluded, "Of Mary, both personally and as a representative figure, we can say she is 'God's workmanship, created in Christ Jesus for good works which God prepared beforehand' (Ephesians 2:10)."

Sources include ARCIC II, *Mary: Grace and Hope in Christ* (London: SPCK / CTS, 2005).

Resources for liturgical use

Service introduction
Mary holds a distinctive place among the people of God, as mother of our Lord. By God's grace, she was enabled to respond to God's word and, by the Holy Spirit, conceive and bring to birth the eternal Word of God in our human flesh. Five other festivals celebrate her place in the life of Christ: on this day we celebrate Mary in her own right, as one truly alive in the glory of God, symbolising our resurrection hope.

Sentence

When the fullness of time had come, God sent his Son, born of a woman, so that we might receive adoption as God's children.

Galatians 4:4–5

Prayer of the day

Loving God,
you chose the blessed virgin Mary
to be the mother of your incarnate Son.
Grant that we, who are redeemed by his blood,
may share with her in the glory of your eternal kingdom,
through Jesus Christ our Lord,
who lives and reigns with you, in the unity of the Holy Spirit,
one God, now and for ever. **Amen.**

or

Heavenly Father,
you chose the virgin Mary, by your grace,
to be the mother of our Lord and Saviour.
Fill us with your grace,
that in all things we may accept your holy will
and with her rejoice in your salvation,
through Jesus Christ our Lord. **Amen.**

Readings

First Evensong:	Psalm 45
	1 Samuel 2:1–10
	Revelation 12:1–6
Morning Prayer:	Psalm 138
	2 Chronicles 7:1–16
	John 2:1–12
Evening Prayer:	Psalm 72
	Songs 2:8–14
	Acts 1:1–14
Main service:	Isaiah 61:10–62:3
	Song of Mary (*APBA* p. 31 or 425) *or* Psalm 113
	Galatians 4:4–7
	Luke 2:1–7

September 2: Martyrs of New Guinea (d. 1942)

AAPB. Prayer and Readings added in *APBA*.

Who were the Martyrs of New Guinea?

Eleven Anglican, 15 Lutheran, 24 Methodist, 188 Roman Catholic and several other Christians were martyred in Papua New Guinea during the Second World War.

In 1941 the Anglican Church in Papua New Guinea celebrated its jubilee. At that time the war with Japan had had little impact, and cooperation between all Christian missions, including German Lutherans, continued. The Japanese entered Rabaul, New Britain on 23 January 1942, and Europeans were evacuated to Australia, but both the Roman Catholic bishop, Alain de Boismeau, and the Anglican bishop, Philip Strong, encouraged their staffs to remain. The centre of government in south-east Papua was evacuated from Samarai to Dogura, the site of the Anglican cathedral.

On 30 January 1942, Bishop Strong made a broadcast to his staff, of which E.C. Rowland says the bishop "felt divinely inspired to give more than just a report":

> I have, from the first, felt that we must endeavour to carry on our work in all circumstances, no matter what the cost may ultimately be to any of us individually. God expects this of us. The Church at home, which sent us out, expects this of us. The Universal Church expects it. The tradition and history of missions requires it of us. Missionaries who have been faithful to the uttermost and are now at

rest are surely expecting it of us. The people whom we serve expect it of us. Our own consciences expect it of us. We would never hold up our faces again, if, for our own safety, we all forsook him and fled when the shadows of the passion began to gather round him in his Spiritual and Mystical Body, the Church in Papua.

The Anglican mission was in the south-east of Papua. Early in March, with invasion likely, the bishop visited all mission stations in *The Maclaren-King* (later commandeered by the Japanese). He had a narrow escape on 10 March when it was fired on by a Japanese seaplane, but all stations were visited and staff encouraged.

The Japanese made their initial landing at Gona on 22 July, and by 3 August had captured Kokoda. Anglican staff at Gona and Sangara were in the immediate path of the invaders and were killed around August 1942.

- The Revd **John Barge** (from Stanthorpe and Toowoomba, Qld) was killed in New Britain in July 1942, though this was not known until 1944. His grave is near Apugi, his station.
- On 7 August, the Revd **Henry Matthews** and Mr **Leslie Gariadi** were killed at sea between Port Moresby and Daru. Matthews was from Ararat, Victoria, had 33 years' ministry in PNG, and was a former Port Moresby rector. Gariadi, a Papuan teacher and evangelist, was Matthews' devoted assistant in Port Moresby, and trained at St Aidan's College, Dogura.
- In early August, Mr **Lucian Tapiedi** was killed by a non-Christian tribe who had captured a group of missionaries from Sangara and Isivita whom he was accompanying to safety. Tapiedi was a Papuan teacher who trained at St Aidan's College, Dogura; his body was found and later reinterred at Sangara. Those with Tapiedi were beheaded soon after on Buna beach. Their bodies were not recovered: it is believed that they were thrown into the sea.

- The Revd **Henry Holland** of Isivita, from NSW, with 42 years' ministry in PNG.
- Mr **John Duffill** of Isivita. From Holy Trinity, Woollongaba, Qld, he was a builder who, though due for furlough, chose to stay in Papua.
- The Revd **Vivian Redlich** insisted on returning to Sangara from sick leave, and held a final Sunday eucharist there before moving into the jungle. A former Bush Brother at Winton, Qld, he was engaged to Sister May Hayman of Gona.
- Sister **Margery Brenchley** of Sangara, a nurse from Holy Trinity, Fortitude Valley, Qld.
- Miss **Lilla Lashmar** of Sangara, a teacher from Adelaide, SA
- In late August, the two Gona missionary Sisters were captured by non-Christian Papuans and handed over to the Japanese — Sister **May Hayman** and Miss **Mavis Parkinson**. The soldiers bayoneted the women and threw their bodies into already dug graves at Jegarata, near Popondetta. Sister Hayman was a nurse from Canberra, ACT, and was engaged to Vivian Redlich. Miss Parkinson, from St Paul's, Ipswich, Qld, was a teacher and a member of the Comrades of St George. Their bodies were recovered after the Japanese had been cleared out of Papua in February 1943 and were reinterred at Sangara.

The decision of the missionaries to stay was criticised in some circles, but after the war it was the missions whose staff had remained who were welcomed back by PNG people.

The commemoration date of 2 September was set at a Synod of PNG in August 1946, together with Prayers and Readings.

Sources include E.C. Rowland, *Faithful unto death. The Story of the New Guinea Martyrs*, from the Project Canterbury website.

Commemorations

Martyrs' Memorial School, now at Agenahambo, PNG.

New Guinea Martyrs', Croydon, Diocese of Melbourne.

Resources for liturgical use

Service introduction

When the Japanese threatened to invade Papua New Guinea in 1942, Bishop Philip Strong encouraged Anglican mission staff to remain at their posts. Eleven Anglicans (Papuans, English and Australians) were martyred, as were 15 Lutherans, 24 Methodists and 188 Roman Catholics. After the war concluded, these missions were welcomed back by locals.

Sentence

Who will separate us from the love of Christ? Will hardship, or distress, or persecution, or famine, or nakedness, or peril, or the sword? No, in all these things we are more than conquerors through him who loved us.

Romans 8:35, 37

Prayers of the day

(Approved by the Anglican Church of PNG in 1946)

O Almighty God, who didst enable thy missionary and Papuan martyrs in New Guinea, in the day of sore trial and danger, to be faithful to their calling and to glorify thee by their deaths: Grant we humbly beseech thee that, by the witness of these thy martyrs, thy whole Church may be enriched and strengthened for thy gathering into thy fold of thy children in all lands; and that we thy servants, following the example of their steadfastness and courage, may labour the more fervently for the coming of thy kingdom, and may so faithfully serve thee here on earth that we may be joined with them hereafter in heaven. Through thy Son Jesus Christ our Lord, who liveth and reigneth with thee and the Holy Ghost, ever one God, world without end. **Amen.**

(As adapted in *APBA*)
All powerful and ever living God,
turn our weakness into strength.
As you gave the martyrs of Papua–New Guinea
the courage to suffer death for Christ,
give us the courage to live in faithful witness to you.
We ask this through Jesus Christ our Lord. **Amen.**

Living God,
you made your Church to grow
through the zeal, courage, and unflinching witness
of your servants martyred in New Guinea.
Give to us and all your people
such steadfast faith in your good purposes
that we may serve faithfully
wherever you have stationed us;
through Jesus Christ our Lord. **Amen.**

Readings

First Evensong:	Psalm 116
	Wisdom 3:1–9
	Revelation 6: 9–11
Morning Prayer:	Psalm 130
	Zephaniah 3:7–20
	Romans 8:18–32
Evening Prayer:	Psalm 126
	Wisdom 5:1–15
	2 Corinthians 6:1–10
Holy Communion:	Zephaniah 3:14–20
	Psalm 130
	Romans 8:33–39
	John 12:20–32

September 3: Eliza Darling, pioneer social reformer in NSW (d. 1868)

New in *APBA*.

Who was Lady Eliza Darling?
Lady Eliza was born Elizabeth Dumaresq in 1798, into a Jersey family of ancient lineage. Her father died when she was six, leading to her growing up in straitened circumstances and being educated at home by her mother. Eliza had an active, enquiring mind and developed lifelong interests in writing, music and art: her brother, Henry Dumaresq, taught her to draw.

In 1817 she married Major General (later Sir) Ralph Darling, acting Governor of Mauritius (1819–23) before serving as Governor of NSW (December 1825–October 1831). Eliza was thus 'first lady' of the Sydney-based colony when William Broughton (see February 20) arrived to shape the Church of England there. She had a child virtually every year, a state of ongoing pregnancy that frequently left her ill. Even so, she taught her children, kept a journal, carried on an extensive correspondence and sustained artistic work.

Her drawings, sent home to England, were so admired by friends that she regretted not having attempted 'a great deal more'. Two watercolours of Sydney harbour and eight of native flowers are extant. She also designed buildings (always with a veranda), furniture and interior decorations. A writer in the July 1829 *Sydney Gazette* noted that she drew "with great beauty and effect" and was "deeply skilled in the minutiae of architectural embellishment". Eliza is listed in the *National Women's Art Book*, and the Design and Art Australia website (www.daao.org.au).

After Sir Ralph's death in 1858, Lady Darling moved to a cottage in Sussex, then a farm in Kent, and finally a country home in East Sussex, shared with her eldest son, the Revd Frederick Darling, and two of her daughters. She endowed one of the buildings as a school for the children of nearby cottagers — an act typical of her lifelong philanthropic involvement, the outcome of her evangelical Christian faith.

Eliza had long shown practical interest in the wellbeing of less fortunate people. In NSW she used her position to turn the Governor's orderlies' stables into the School House for the Girls' School of Industry. She assisted the women convicts in the Female Factory, patronised the Benevolent Society and Sydney Dispensary, and actively supported the Sunday School movement.

Eliza died on 3 September 1868 and is buried in the churchyard of St Mary the Virgin, Hartfield, East Sussex. A devoted wife and mother, her warm, firm ways helped sustain close family relationships. She is remembered for her devout, practical and creative Christian faith in circumstances of considerable ambiguity.

Sources include the biographical outline by Brian Fletcher and Joan Kerr on the *Design and Art Australia* website.

Resources for liturgical use

Service introduction
Eliza Darling, née Dumaresq, lived out her Christian faith as the 'First Lady' of the early NSW colony, and later as a widow in England. She is remembered for her artistic skill, and for her practical and creative Christian faith in circumstances of considerable ambiguity.

Sentence

She who has clean hands and a pure heart, who does not lift up her soul to what is false, will receive blessing from the Lord, and vindication from the God of her salvation.

Psalm 24:4, 5

Prayer of the day

(Adapted from 'For a Saint' in *APBA*)
Faithful God,
you have surrounded us with a great cloud of witnesses.
Grant that we, empowered by your creative grace,
and encouraged by the example of your servant Eliza Darling,
may be faithful and creative in our personal relationships,
and in public life demonstrate our faith by
performing the good works you give us,
through Jesus Christ, the pioneer and perfector of our faith. **Amen.**

Readings

Proverbs 8:1–3, 12–21
Psalm 15
Philippians 4:4–9
Matthew 6:26–33

September 11: Mother Esther CHN, founder of the Community of the Holy Name, a religious community in Melbourne (d. 1931)

New in *APBA*.

Who was Mother Esther?

Emma Caroline Silcock was born in 1858 in Norfolk, England, but not baptised until 1877, having come to Christian faith under the influence of the Anglo-catholic movement. In 1884 she entered the Community of St Mary the Virgin, Wantage, as Novice Esther Emma, spending a year in London's slums until a back injury saw her sent to Melbourne to recuperate. She found her life's work in the growing city's sordid 'streets and lanes'.

The 1850s gold rush led to Melbourne's population growing quickly, but by the 1880s much of the city area was a slum. The Mission to Streets and Lanes opened in 1885 in an old baker's shop. Other missions sought to help individuals, but this Mission, initiated by Anglicans of Anglo-catholic sympathies, sought to work in a more social way, having a Christian community at its heart, and concentrating on the city community. The arrival of Sister Esther was the catalyst for MSL adopting its community ethos.

The small community moved from the baker's shop to a former dance theatre, with Esther as Mother Foundress of the Community of the Holy Name. She had been in Melbourne only a year or so when she was authorised to take care of "the friendless and uncared for" under the *Neglected Children's Act*. The numbers involved called for a home: by 1892 a Brighton property had been purchased for a children's home, with a babies' home soon added. The same year saw a home for wayward or incorrigible girls established, in the 'quiet country village' of Cheltenham, which worked with the courts. Each facility was supervised by Sisters, some of whom trained as nurses, and a chapel enabled worship to form the central focus.

The monastic element of CHN had raised suspicions, and in 1890 Bishop Goe admitted MSL's sisters as deaconesses. Esther chose not to join them, but seek monastic vows from Wantage, which eventuated in 1894, after which women who joined her were professed privately by the bishop's chaplain before being admitted as deaconesses. In 1898 the sisters designated Esther as Mother, and in March 1912 Bishop Lowther Clarke gave the nine professed sisters a charter for the Community of the Holy Name. The evidently apostolic work of the sisters won widespread support across the Diocese of Melbourne. From 1890 St Paul's Cathedral allocated its Good Friday alms to the Mission, and the Governor's wife agreed to lay the foundation stone of a new children's home not long after.

In 1911 the sisters operated St George's Intermediate Hospital in Kew: a maternity ward was added in 1925 and an X-ray unit in 1930. This not only gained an excellent reputation, but (despite modest fees) ran at a profit because it was nearly always full. Together with St Ives Private Hospital in East Melbourne, this assisted middle-income earners who could not afford hospital, but were ineligible for the public hospitals treating the poor.

The Fitzroy Mission Home, opened in 1912, was not only a community base for the MSL community, but a centre of community life, with boys' and girls' clubs, a weekly mothers meeting, dispensary for the poor, clothing sales, soup kitchens, milk money ... and Sunday evening services. Volunteers, local priests, students and doctors gave help, so that a 'systemic' approach to a particular person's need could be taken. In the 1920s the Mission was involved with two inner-city schools, until they closed, and prepared children for confirmation.

The sisters worked long hours on basic support, as part of a close community led by Mother Esther. By 1929 there were 25 sisters, five novices and a postulant in the Community of the Holy Name. Auxiliaries were set up across Melbourne diocese, giving both material and personal support — 32 existed by 1932, with some 56 parishes giving help — and two homes were managed in Newcastle diocese.

When the Depression came, the Mission offered one of the few effective responses made by the churches, and successive Anglican archbishops lent their support and gave recognition. As well as general relief for those in need — given out as soon as it came in — work for desperate men was sought, concentrated on locals known to the Sisters, in order to maintain a community focus. This also meant that when they appeared in court, did probation work, visited Pentridge prison or the Women's Hospital (where they regularly baptised babies), the Sisters were known, and knew the people involved.

Mother Esther emphasised that all work must be done for the love of Jesus, otherwise it would be barren and of little value. One of her favourite sayings was, "The future is in the hands of God who loves us." She began the Community's Rule as follows:

> The aim and object of this Community into which these Sisters have been called, is twofold. First, the Glory of God and the perfection of those He calls out of the world to serve Him in the Religious Life, under the perpetual vows of Poverty, Chastity and Obedience. Second, the Community has been founded for active Mission work in the Church for the honour and love of our Blessed Lord Jesus Christ.

Mother Esther continued to be the inspiration for a vibrant ministry. When she died after a short illness on 11 September 1931, the Mission was able to carry on and expand.

Sources include notes prepared by Barbara Darling for the Trinity Certificate.

Commemoration

When a new Community House was established in Cheltenham in 1935, it was built as a memorial to Mother Esther.

Resources for liturgical use

Service introduction

Emma Silcock was baptised in England as an adult, and entered the Community of St Mary the Virgin. In 1885, aged 27, she came to Melbourne for health reasons, and was drawn into work with the poor in its 'streets and lanes'. As Mother Esther, she founded the Community of the Holy Name, in which she served for four decades, and saw its ministry accepted across the diocese.

Sentence

You, Lord, are all that I have; I have promised to keep your word. I have sought your favour with all my heart; be gracious to me according to your promise.

Psalm 119:57–58

Prayer of the day
(Adapted from 'For a Monastic' in *APBA*)
O God,
your blessed Son Jesus Christ became poor
so that through his poverty many might become rich.
Inspired by the devotion of your servant Mother Esther,
may we serve you with singleness of heart,
and support those in need as our sisters and brothers.
Delivered from inordinate love of this world,
may we attain to the riches of the age to come,
your new creation in Jesus Christ our Lord. **Amen.**

Readings
Micah 6:6–8 *or* Acts 2:42–47a
Psalm 119:161–168 *or* Psalm 133
Matthew 6:24–33
2 Corinthians 6:1–10 *or* 2 Corinthians 8:7–15

September 15: John Oliver Feetham, bishop and bush brother (d. 1947)

New in *APBA*.

Who was Bishop Feetham?
John Oliver Feetham was born in 1873 into an English vicarage family, whose sons spread across the professions, from the military to the arts. Schooled at Marlborough College (1886–92), he went on to read mathematics at Trinity Hall, Cambridge (1892–95). After graduation he lived at Oxford Hall in Bethnal Green in London's slums, working as a lay minister, before entering Wells Theological College. Ordained deacon in 1899 and priest in 1900, he served his curacy in Bethnal Green — this East London experience shaped lifelong concern for those in need. Alongside this, he admired British 'public school' education, which served as his model in establishing schools in North Queensland.

In 1902 Fredrick Campion had gone to Australia to found the Brotherhood of the Good Shepherd, a community of single clergy of Anglo-catholic persuasion who took vows to serve in the outback. Feetham followed Campion out to NSW in 1907, committing himself to ministry among the people of the Australian bush: he became the second Principal of the Brotherhood. An invitation to Townsville to conduct a clergy retreat led to his being elected Bishop of North Queensland in October 1912: he would remain as bishop until 1947, spanning crucial years in the development of the region. He supported conscription in 1916 and 1917, and was a strong proponent of the allied cause in both World Wars, as well as having sustained engagement with government over several decades.

Feetham contributed much to the spread of Christian faith in the outback, especially through the Brotherhood, whose clergy he inspired to see the people of the bush as epitomising Australian virtues. He was successful in gaining financial support from the pastoral companies, a mark of the influence of this outlook. As a priest in NSW, Feetham had marked differences with Archbishop Wright of Sydney: under his influence North Queensland became one of the most uniformly Anglo-catholic, as well as one of most lively, Australian Anglican dioceses.

As bishop, Feetham sought to replicate the British public school system, so that rural Queensland children could have the best of the British and Christian traditions: 'Church and Empire' was his motto. He invested enormous personal effort into these schools, bringing Sister Emma SSA from Brisbane (see March 9) to found St Anne's, Townsville in 1917, and then All Souls and St Gabriel's, Charters Towers: the Christian influence of these schools continues. (St Mary's, Herberton, closed in 1966.)

Feetham's personal influence across the region of his huge diocese, especially among the clergy, was incalculable. Over six feet tall and often showing white socks between his trousers and shoes, he usually refused to sleep in a bed, and drove 'Ermintrude', an early model Ford, with panache. Feetham "infected others with his own enthusiasm, and his personality, into which his Christianity was fully integrated, was colourful, attractive and eccentric" (Alison Moore, *ADB*).

After World War II Feetham experienced ongoing illness, and in 1946 went to Brisbane for surgery. He announced his resignation from the diocese as from 30 September 1947, but died in Townsville on 14 September 1947.

Sources include Alison Moore, 'John Feetham' entry, *ADB*.

Commemorations

John Oliver Feetham Church, Cardwell was consecrated on 15 September 2002, following its rebuilding after being devastated by Cyclone Yasi.

Feetham House, as All Souls'/St Gabriel School, Charters Towers.

Feetham Street, St James' retirement village, Townsville.

Resources for liturgical use

Service introduction

John Oliver Feetham, a young English priest, in 1907 responded to the call to minister in Australia's outback, initially in western NSW. He soon found himself leading the Brotherhood of the Good Shepherd, and in 1912 was elected Bishop of North Queensland. A colourful eccentric, for over 35 years Feetham traversed his huge diocese in 'Ermintrude', an old Ford. Much loved by his clergy, he fostered Christian faith through the schools he founded, and is remembered across Queensland as a pioneer of the gospel.

Sentences

Keep watch over yourselves and over all the flock, of which the Holy Spirit has made you overseers, to shepherd the church of God that he obtained with the blood of his own Son.

Acts 20:28–29

Teach the Lord's words to your children, talking about them when you are at home and when you are away, when you lie down and when you rise.

Deuteronomy 11:19–20

Prayer of the day
(Adapted from 'For a Bishop' in *APBA*)
O God, our heavenly Father,
you raised up your faithful servant John Oliver Feetham
to be a bishop in your Church
and to feed your flock in outback Queensland.
We thank you for his love of the bush,
his leadership of the Brotherhood of the Good Shepherd,
and his vision for the education of children.
Give abundantly to all pastors and teachers
the gifts of your Holy Spirit,
so that they may minister in your household
as true servants of Christ
and stewards of your holy mysteries,
through Jesus Christ our Lord. **Amen.**

Readings
Isaiah 42:10–16 *or* Acts 20:28–36
Psalm 119:9–16
2 Corinthians 5:11–20
Matthew 28:16–20 *or* John 21:15–17

September 18: John Ramsden Wollaston, priest and missionary of Western Australia (d. 1856)

New in *APBA*.

Who was John Wollaston?

John Ramsden Wollaston was born in London in 1791 into a family with strong school ties. He went to Charterhouse School, where his father was a master, and his mother's father had been headmaster. After graduating from Christ's College, Cambridge in 1812, he was ordained, serving in West Wickham, Cambridgeshire. In 1819 he married Mary Amelia Gledstones: they would have five sons and two daughters, the support of whom was a challenge for his stipend.

In 1840, looking to secure his family's future, he applied to be Chaplain for the Western Australian Land Company, a speculative attempt at a new settlement at Australind. Amid confusion about his status, Wollaston took the family to the new colony, only to find that no stipend was available — the venture was near collapse, largely due to its isolation. The Governor, John Hutt, offered to pay a stipend on condition that a church building was erected. So Wollaston and his sons bought land with a dilapidated whalers' cottage, and built a small timber chapel, opened in September 1842. It remains the second oldest church in the state, later consecrated as St Mark's and now located in Picton, WA.

Wollaston is remembered less for this church than for his sustained energy in promoting the gospel in the Swan River colony: "his continued labours as a parish priest earned him the name of a 'worthy, laborious, energetic, excellent missionary'" (G.C. Bolton, *ADB*). In

February 1842 he brought together the five Church of England clergy in Perth. They assessed the church's problems, drew up a statement and called on the Bishop of Australia, William Broughton (see February 20), to visit. The request was denied, and Wollaston could not convince the other clergy to meet annually.

In 1849 the new Governor, Charles Fitzgerald, moved Wollaston to the significant port of Albany. Bishop Short and Archdeacon Hale of the new diocese of Adelaide (which then included Western Australia) visited the colony soon afterwards. Short, impressed with Wollaston's commitment and skills, appointed him Archdeacon of Western Australia, a position he held until his death in 1856. Wollaston travelled extensively, always on horseback, completing five visitations to the state's settled areas.

Significant growth in population, not least due to convict transportation, saw new challenges arise; Church of England clergy were called on to serve Nonconformists without ministers. Wollaston met this situation successfully, doubling clergy numbers to ten; in 1851 he established a mission to Aboriginal people; and in 1853 drafted an Act that regulated church property affairs. His ultimate aim was to secure a bishop for Western Australia. A scheme for settlers to donate land for a see had limited success, but by 1854 plans were in place for Archdeacon Hale to become the first Bishop of Perth (in 1857). Sadly, before Hale could be in place, Wollaston, aged 65, died on 3 May 1856 of a cerebral haemorrhage due to exhaustion.

Wollaston's journals show him to be an observant commentator on colonial manners, and "a man whose qualities of humility, common sense and devoted perseverance enabled him to give purpose and order to a very isolated branch of the Anglican communion" (Bolton, *ADB*).

Sources include G.C. Bolton, 'John Ramsden Wollaston' entry, *ADB*.

Commemorations

John Wollaston Theological College, Perth, WA (established 1957), now part of the Wollaston Conference Centre.

John Wollaston Anglican Community School, Kelmscott, WA.

The suburb of Wollaston in Bunbury, WA. A plaque in St John's, Albany has these words:

> Sacred to the memory of Archdeacon Wollaston,
> who died May 3rd 1856 aged 65 years.
> This tablet is erected by his congregation in grateful remembrance
> of his zeal in promoting the temporal interest of this church and of
> his earnest solicitude for the spiritual welfare of his people.

Resources for liturgical use

Service introduction

John Ramsden Wollaston came to Western Australia in 1840 to minister in a new settlement. When it failed, Wollaston built a chapel from which to minister. His initiative saw him appointed to Albany, and then made Archdeacon of Western Australia. His sustained travels saw an Aboriginal mission established, clergy numbers double, and Perth getting a bishop. But Wollaston died of exhaustion, aged 65, just months before this took place. He is remembered as "a worthy, laborious, energetic, excellent missionary".

Sentence

The love of Christ urges us on, because we are convinced that one has died for all, so that those who live might live no longer for themselves, but for him who died and was raised for them.

2 Corinthians 5:14–15

Prayer of the day
(From the Diocese of Perth)
Almighty God,
you called John Ramsden Wollaston to preach the Gospel
amongst the early settlers in Western Australia.
Grant that we may so follow his example,
and obey your will for us,
that with confidence in your grace
we may effectively proclaim the Gospel in our own day,
through Jesus Christ our Lord,
who lives and reigns with you and the Holy Spirit,
ever one God, world without end. **Amen.**

Readings
Ezekiel 37:1–14 *or* Isaiah 52:7–10
Psalm 103:15–22
Acts 14:21–28 *or* 2 Corinthians 4:7–15
Mark 1:1–8

September 20: John Coleridge Patteson, first bishop of Melanesia, martyr (d. 1871)

AAPB and *APBA*.

Who was Bishop Patteson?

John Coleridge Patteson was born in London in 1827 of well-to-do parents. He was educated at a private school in Devon and then at Eton, where he proved to be a good student and sportsman. Deeply religious, in 1845 he went to Oxford and was influenced by the Oxford Movement, though he never became a 'party member'. Patteson studied briefly in Germany, where he became competent in Hebrew and Arabic and showed his outstanding flair for languages.

Ordained deacon in 1853 and priest the following year, he offered himself to Bishop Selwyn (see April 11) for work in Melanesia. He arrived in New Zealand in 1855. Two years later he was put in charge of the Melanesian Mission, and on 24 February 1861 was consecrated as the first Bishop of Melanesia. Like Selwyn, Patteson was a new style of bishop: a missionary, at the forefront of the Church's work, boldly leading into new areas rather than ministering to a settled diocese. It was a conception of the episcopate that caused debate in England, where the action of a Church of England bishop operating beyond the boundaries of British rule seemed strange, if not illegal.

Patteson inherited the system established by Selwyn, in which young men and women from the islands were taken to Auckland for instruction during the summer. They then returned to their islands, in the hope that they would provide Christian influence in their communities. It was not very successful: Patteson determined that missionary work must be done in the islands themselves and in one of the Melanesian languages.

The ten years of Patteson's episcopate were spent opening up the Melanesia islands to the gospel, and arranging for the education of young Melanesians, first at Kohimarama in Auckland, then from a base on Mota in the Banks Group, and from 1867 on Norfolk Island. One of his objects was to establish a group of Melanesian priests. This in itself was a novel idea. He was a brilliant linguist, but his greatest gift was that of friendship. He had no sense of prejudice about colour at all and, although he realised that the Melanesians seemed uncivilised, he had a clear vision of what they might become.

Patteson seemed freer than most of his European contemporaries from the 19th century view of Melanesian life as something to be replaced with Christianity. He was convinced that the Melanesians could accept and practise Christianity within their own culture. He wrote: "No Melanesian is excluded now from any position of trust … Some day Melanesian bishops may preside over native churches throughout the islands of the sea."

Travel in Melanesia was always risky, Patteson's life was often in danger and his health suffered in the 1860s. In the same period there grew up a considerable labour trade, as entrepreneurs in Australia and Fiji sought cheap indentured labour from Melanesia. While many Melanesians were enthusiastic travellers, some labour traders were unscrupulous and even used Patteson's name to lure people on to their ships. Missionaries in particular opposed the trade, in part because it disturbed their own operations.

On 20 September 1871 Patteson was murdered on the island of Nukapu. Joseph Atkin and Stephen Taroaniara, who accompanied Patteson, died a week later of wounds received at the time. It was widely believed that Patteson's death was in retaliation for 'slave' trading, but this is not certain. His death did, however, ensure more rigorous regulations on labour recruiting, and gave strong impetus in England to the missionary work of the Church. What is most remembered is Patteson's attitude that his life was taken by those for whom he would gladly have given it.

Notes based on *For All the Saints*, Lectionary resources for the Anglican Church in Aoteroa New Zealand: www.anglican.org.nz/Resources/Lectionary-and-Worship/For-All-the-Saints/For-All-the-Saints.

Resources for liturgical use

Sentence
In the day of my distress I will call, O Lord, and surely you will answer me.
                                                            Psalm 86:7

Prayer of the day
God of the southern isles and seas,
we remember with thanksgiving your servant John Patteson,
whose life was taken by those
for whom he would freely have given it.
Grant us the same courage in extending your gospel,
and readiness to share our life with others,
for the sake of Jesus Christ our Redeemer. **Amen.**

Readings
Hosea 11:1–4
Psalm 116
2 Corinthians 4:5–12
Mark 8:31–35

November 2: All Souls

Not in *BCP*. Lesser Festival in *AAPB*.
Prayer and Readings added in *APBA*.

Why All Souls' as well as All Saints' Days?
All Souls' Day is in many ways an extension of All Saints' Day. In some ways this might be thought of as a mistake, since originally All Saints' Day was the day on which Christians remembered with gratitude and love all those who had gone before them in the faith of Christ. As 'saint' came to be restricted to the heroes of the faith, the urge to commemorate all the members of the church who had died in the faith of Christ found its outlet in the development of All Souls' Day.

The festival was formalised in 998 by the Abbot of Cluny, Odilo, who set the day after All Saints' Day to commemorate "all the dead who have existed from the beginning of the world to the end of time". As Cluny's reforming influence spread through other monasteries, the observance of All Souls' Day grew across Europe and then beyond. It was abolished in the Church of England at the Reformation because of its association with masses for the dead, payment for which led to widespread abuses.

Over the past century the day has been gradually restored to calendars across the Anglican Communion, as a commemoration of the faithful who have departed this life in Christ. Events such as the Great War saw people looking for a way to remember before God those who died with little attachment to the Church. In recent decades this time of year has also come to be associated with services, in places such as hospitals or worksites, where those who have died in the year past are remembered in the presence of God.

The reference in the Great Thanksgiving prayer to our joining in the praise of God with "all the company of heaven" echoes the hope-filled truth proclaimed on All Souls' Day.

Notes

a) In the New Testament, believers are not said to 'die', but to 'fall asleep': it is Christ who died so that those who trust in him may live. The expression is not a euphemism to avoid speaking of unpleasant realities, but reflects the assurance which Christian hope brings.

b) So 'souls' in the feast's name does not mean the non-material aspect of being human, but has the classical English sense of referring to the whole person.

c) The Sentence, prayer and Readings for this day, consistent with the funeral resources in APBA, focus on the Christian hope of resurrection. They avoid speculation both about the 'intermediate state' of those who have 'fallen asleep' in Christ, and the ultimate fate of those who are not Christian believers.

Commemoration
All Souls' School, Charters Towers, Queensland.

Several parish churches in Australia, and elsewhere.

Resources for liturgical use

Service introduction
All Saints' Day originally celebrated all believers, but 'saint' gradually came to refer to a hero of the faith, and then to those in a position to intercede for others, 'patron saints'. Around 1000 AD a French abbot initiated a commemoration of all believers on the following day, All

Souls' Day. This tradition spread across the church, though it was abolished at the Reformation since it had become associated with masses for the dead. Its restoration in *APBA* reflects the Christian hope of resurrection in the face of death.

Sentence

"I am the resurrection and the life," says the Lord. "Whoever lives and believes in me shall never die."

John 11:25, 26

Prayer of the day

We thank you, loving God,
for all your servants, known to us and unknown,
who have departed this life in your faith and fear.
Give us grace so to follow their good examples,
that with them we may be brought to a joyful resurrection,
and be made partakers of your heavenly kingdom,
through Jesus Christ our Lord,
who lives and reigns with you and the Holy Spirit,
one God, for ever and ever. **Amen.**

Readings

Job 14:1–14 *or* Job 19:21–27
Psalm 29 *or* Psalm 90
Romans 6:3–9
John 5:19–29

November 25: James Noble, pioneer Aboriginal deacon (d. 1941)

APBA — description revised, General Synod 2001.

Who was James Noble?

James Noble was born around 1876 near Boulia, North Queensland, and in his teens was a stockman with the Doyle brothers, becoming a superb horseman. He moved south with the brothers to Invermien, near Scone, NSW, and gained an education through evening lessons. He was baptised at St Luke's, Scone on 1 July 1895 and confirmed six days later.

Ill health saw James return to Queensland, where from 1896 he assisted the Revd E.R. Gribble (son of the Revd John Gribble), at Yarrabah, an Anglican mission near Cairns. Noble's effectiveness in ministry saw him licensed on 11 October 1901 as a lay reader in the parish of St John's, Cairns. In 1904 he helped resettle some hundred Aborigines from Fraser Island at Yarrabah.

Soon after his arrival at Yarrabah, James married Maggie Frew, but their son died within months, followed soon after by Maggie. A year later he became engaged to Lizzie Moore, the first matron of Yarrabah hospital, but she also died. James later married Angelina from Winton: she had been sent to Yarrabah by the Cairns police, after she had been abducted by a horse dealer (who dressed her in men's clothing and called her 'Tommy').

In 1904 Angelina accompanied James on an expedition to the Mitchell River to help choose a mission site. The couple looked after the party, and negotiated with local Aborigines warring with encroaching cattlemen: the venture led to James taking on increasing responsibilities in ministry. In 1905 he was given charge of 30 Aborigines farming at Bukki Creek, largest of the Yarrabah mission's eight outstations; in 1907 he represented Gribble at the Diocese of North Queensland synod; 1908 saw him preach and speak to large gatherings in Brisbane; and in 1909 James and Angelina pioneered the Roper River mission.

In 1913 Gribble asked the couple to reopen the mission at Forrest River, on Western Australia's Cambridge Gulf. Finding it in poor condition, James constructed several buildings, including one where Angelina treated the sick. He was licensed as a Lay Reader at Forrest River in February 1925, and in May Gribble sent him to preach and speak across the eastern states. On 13 September 1925 he was ordained deacon at St George's Cathedral, Perth, before returning to Forrest River — the first Aboriginal Anglican clergyman in Australia. By 1928 the Forrest River mission had 24 buildings, many constructed of sun-dried bricks made by James. In 1933 the permanent population of Aborigines was 170, with some 800 regular visitors. In addition to nursing, Angelina taught children, baked bread and cooked for the staff.

In August 1926 reports appeared of police reprisals for the spearing of an overseer on a cattle station. Gribble sent Noble, skilled in tracking, to investigate. At the site of one of the massacres he discovered an improvised oven: the teeth and charred bones he brought back, together with his evidence before a Commission of Inquiry in 1927, contributed to the arrest of two policemen for murder. Angelina, who knew at least five Aboriginal languages, interpreted for the inquiry.

James and Angelina returned to Yarrabah in 1932, before going with Gribble to Palm Island, where James was licensed as assistant minister on 19 December 1933. But with his health declining, the family came back to Yarrabah in 1934, where James visited the hospital and taught traditional skills. He died on 25 November 1941 after a fall, and was buried in Yarrabah cemetery. Angelina died on 19 October 1964 at Yarrabah, where she also was buried. Two sons and four daughters survived them.

Gribble claimed James Noble as a gifted speaker whose earnest, unassuming manner "completely won all with whom he came in contact".

Sources include Jan Kociumbas, 'James Noble' entry, *ADB*.

Resources for liturgical use

Service introduction
James Noble grew up as an Aboriginal stockman in Queensland. From his baptism and confirmation as a young man onwards, he sustained a Christian ministry of growing responsibilities. He was ordained deacon in 1925. Based at Yarrabah, near Cairns, James and his wife Angelina pioneered mission stations across northern Australia. They helped bring justice for Aboriginal people after police reprisals, and set a public example of practical holy living.

Sentence
To all to whom I send you, you shall go, and whatever I command you, you shall speak.

Jeremiah 1:7

Prayer of the day
(New, using phrases from *APBA*)
God of holy dreaming,
we thank you for your servant James Noble,
whom you called to bring the gospel
to the Aboriginal peoples of northern Australia.
We thank you for his ministry with Angelina
as an evangelist, pioneer and deacon.
Raise up men and women in this land
who live out your reign of peace,
so that the whole world may know
the love of God in Christ Jesus our Lord. **Amen.**

Readings:
Isaiah 2:1–5
1 Timothy 3:8–16
Psalm 96
Luke 10:1–9

December 2: Frances Perry, founder of the Royal Women's Hospital, Melbourne (d. 1892)

New in *APBA*.

Who was Frances Perry?

Frances ('Fanny', as she signed herself) Perry was born on 16 June 1814 and baptised on 21 July at the Fish Street Independent Chapel, Kingston-upon-Hull, Yorkshire. Through her brother John at the University of Cambridge, Fanny met Charles Perry, curate at a nearby parish: they married on 14 October 1841, but had no children. The couple shared a firm evangelical faith, an interest in biblical scholarship and missionary work.

Charles Perry accepted the new bishopric of Melbourne in 1847 (see February 20): he and Frances left England in October on the *Stag*. The new bishop led services on the ship and taught Greek to the clergy going out with him, while Frances took scripture classes for the women and practised her benevolence on the steerage passengers.

The party reached Port Phillip on 23 January 1848, then just a dozen years since its being founded. They immediately set out on their task, to advance the Church of England in the new colony of Victoria in both public and private spheres. Frances coped with demanding work as Charles' personal assistant, while coping with the expectations of local gentry: she was recalled by Mary Stawell as "a lively good little woman, nothing very particular as a companion, and has a good deal of English wit or kitten liveliness". She especially disliked tea meetings: "I cannot help considering them useful things, but I get dreadfully tired, and shirk them whenever I can" (Sherlock, *ADB*).

Frances accompanied Charles on long journeys through his huge diocese, riding, walking, and staying in rough quarters. She wrote copiously about the country she found herself in — its flora and fauna, the Snowy Mountains, the heat, flies, bushfires and discovery of gold. Her colourful letters were published under the pseudonym 'Richard Perry', and show a detailed interest in the people and landscapes she encountered.

She is best remembered for her sustained work on behalf of women, especially as the population of Victoria grew rapidly after gold was discovered. She took leading roles in the Governesses' Home, the Carlton Refuge, and the Melbourne Orphan Asylum. Her sustained philanthropy and position as bishop's wife placed her in the public realm, but she deferred to male authority and confined herself to women's welfare.

Frances' chief work was as founding president of the Melbourne Lying-in and Infirmary for Diseases of Women and Children (now Royal Women's) Hospital, from 1856 to 1874. After the Melbourne Hospital declined to set up a midwifery section, she helped negotiate the new institution's establishment with two local doctors and a Ladies' Committee (supported by a smaller Gentlemen's Committee). Several of those involved were evangelical Christians: the first version of the Rules drawn up by the Ladies' Committee stated that the hospital would run according to "the principles of the Christian Religion as these are received by the various Evangelical branches of the Protestant Church". Morning and evening prayers were to be read by the Matron, including appeals to the Creator for mercy, pity and forgiveness for suffering (viewed as a consequence of sin). Frances took a sustained interest in the Hospital's work, espousing moral and domestic purity, monitoring the marital status of patients and regularly inspecting the wards.

After the Perrys left Melbourne in 1874 to retire in London, Frances maintained her correspondence with colonial acquaintances, and continued to take a keen interest in church affairs. After Charles died in 1891, she moved near her brother John, vicar of Kendal. She died exactly one year after Charles, on 2 December 1892.

Sources include Peter Sherlock, 'Frances Perry' entry, *ADB*; Australian Christian heroes website; and National Portrait Gallery biography (online); Elizabeth Rushen, *Bishopscourt Melbourne: Family Home and Official Residence* (Melbourne: Mosaic / Morningstar, 2013).

Commemorations
Frances Perry House, Royal Women's Hospital, Melbourne (opened 1970).

Resources for liturgical use

Service introduction
Frances Perry came from England in 1848 as the wife of Charles Perry, first Bishop of Melbourne. She was tireless in supporting his ministry, travelling extensively with him to establish and build up churches across Victoria. Her initiatives in caring for women and children in the new colony led to the establishment of what is now the Royal Women's Hospital, whose Frances Perry House perpetuates her memory.

Sentence
Religion that is pure and undefiled before God, the Father, is this: to care for orphans and widows in their distress, and to keep oneself unstained by the world.

James 1:27

Prayer of the day
(Adapted from 'For a Saint' in *APBA*)
Faithful God,
you have surrounded us with a great cloud of witnesses.
Grant that we,
encouraged by the example of your servant Frances Perry,
may persevere in caring for women in need,
and supporting the ministry of bishops and other pastors.
Like her, may we run the race that is set before us,
until at last with her we attain to your eternal joy,
through Jesus Christ, the pioneer and perfector of our faith. **Amen.**

Readings
Proverbs 31:10–31
Psalm 1
Acts 9:36–42
John 11:20–27

www.ingramcontent.com/pod-product-compliance
Lightning Source LLC
Chambersburg PA
CBHW030447300426
44112CB00009B/1200